BRAINWAVES

INVASION BRITAIN

Kevin Jane

Folens Publishers

Published by Folens Limited, Dunstable and Dublin

Folens Limited, Albert House, Apex Business Centre, Boscombe Road, Dunstable, LU5 4RL, England

Acknowledgements

The author wishes to thank the following people for their time and encouragement in producing this book:

Paul Nicholls, the illustrator, a friend and colleague who understood exactly the 'soul' of the cultures and who was able to interpret my ideas with his super line drawings.

Jean Pollard who read and provided ideas for some units of work and shook her head when the activity being reviewed seemed 'thin'!

My wife Julie and daughter Stephanie who gave me the time to write up the material.

Finally, this book is dedicated to the children of Connor Downs County Primary School, Cornwall, by their headteacher.

Maps:

Jillian Luff of Bitmap Graphics.

Cover Photographs:

Michael Holford photographs Limited.	(Top)
Corinium Museum.	(Centre)
Reproduced by Courtesy of the Trustees of the British Museum.	(Bottom)

Folens books are protected by international copyright laws. All rights reserved. The copyright of all materials in this book, except where otherwise stated, remains the property of the publisher and author(s). No part of this publication may be reproduced, stored in a retrieval system, or transmitted, in any form or by any means, for whatever purpose, without the written permission of Folens Limited.

Folens do allow photocopying of selected pages of this publication for educational use, providing that this use is within the confines of the purchasing institution. You may make as many copies as you require for classroom use of the pages so marked.

This resource may be used in a variety of ways; however it is not intended that teachers or students should write directly into the book itself.

© 1990 Folens Limited, on behalf of the author.

First published 1990 by Folens Limited, Albert House, Apex Business Centre, Boscombe Road, Dunstable, LU5 4RL, England.

ISBN 1 85276 064 8

Folens COPYMASTER

Printed in Great Britain by Hollen Street Press.

Contents

	How do we Know?	9
Celts Unit	Celtic Homes	10
	Celtic Craftsmen	11
	Celtic Technology	12
	Lindow Man - A Mystery	13
	What did the Celts Look Like?	14
	Boudicca's Revolt!	15
	Celtic Art	16
	Four Seasons	17
	Hill Fort	18
	Figures in the Landscape	19
Romans Unit	Invasion Britian	20
	Legionary	21
	Town Planner	22
	Roman Villa	23
	Roman Roads	24
	Curses!	25
	A Roman Wall Painting	26
Saxons Unit	Sea Wolves!	27
	Sutton Hoo: Part 1	28
	Sutton Hoo: Part 2	29
	Saxon and Viking Writing	30
	Anglo Saxon Riddles	31
	Life in an Anglo Saxon Village	32
	Don't burn the Cakes!	33
	The Last Anglo Saxon King: 1042 - 1066	34
Vikings Unit	Viking Attack on Lindisfarne!	35
	Viking Ship	36
	Traders and Craftsmen	37
	The Viking World	38
	Viking Dress	39
	Your Move Snarri!	40
	Ship Shapes	41
	Viking Homes	42
	A Viking Feast!	43
	Viking Picture Stones	44
Normans Unit	Countdown to Invasion 1066	45
	Invasion 1066!	46
	Saxon versus Norman: Hastings 1066	47
	Putting it in the Right Order	48

© 1990 Folens Limited

Teachers Notes

Introduction

The material contained within this book is based upon the invading people of the British Isles. It includes resource material for the Celts, the Romans, the Saxons, the Vikings and Normans. The material in part is guided by the Key Stage 2, Core History Study Unit 2: Invaders and Settlers - The Romans, Anglo Saxons and Vikings in Britian, but not exclusively so. It would be difficult to study the Romans without the context of the Celtic culture they found here. That culture is rich and diverse, and still found today in Scotland, Ireland, Wales and the West Country. Similarly, the Saxon story is not complete without the exciting episodes that led to the Norman invasion in 1066.

It must be emphasised that the material found here is not intended to be used as a course of study of these cultures. There is not enough room within this format to provide a complete and comprehensive study of any one individual culture. Rather, it is used by teachers to support, extend and enrich historical work that may be subject discipline led but preferably in support of cross-curricular thematic work. It is also intended that the material be used by groups or pairs of children as required by teachers, and not always the whole class.

The role of the teacher in using this material is fundamental. Much of the material requires an oral introduction and follow-up work and demands that reference material be at the children's disposal where necessary.

The resource material is divided up into units which entitles the children to appreciate the culture of those peoples and provides an access to their 'story'. That culture is then reflected in a cross-curricular approach. The units draw upon the literature, art, technology, geography and history of the period to enhance children's understanding and appreciation of the past. The material is designed to be interactive - it will demand and promote discussion, opinion, attitude forming and decision making.

The units are content led but are designed to develop key historical concepts and skills so that they work in the manner of the historian. Whenever possible the units draw upon evidence from documents, physical sources or artefacts which are fundamental to the study of history. It should be understood that evidence is always incomplete. Therefore, what we know of the distant past is always speculative until more evidence is discovered.

It is to be hoped that teachers will look beyond the format of an A4 photocopiable sheet and design work around the activities presented here. The idea is that literature, drama, art, music, experimental archaeology, design technology and historical site visits will fully develop the children's understanding of their cultural roots and shared inheritance.

To complement the units teachers will find brief notes on:

- the purpose behind the activity
- the focus of the activity, additional information and ideas for extensions or follow-up
- the Attainment Target it aims to satisfy and the 4 dimensions of historical knowledge - Political; Economic; Technological and Scientific; Social and Religious; Cultural and Aesthetic.

Kevin Jane.

© 1990 Folens Limited

Title	Purpose	Focus/Information/Extensions	AT & PESC
How do we Know?	To appreciate that knowledge and understanding of the past is based on the informed guess work of *evidence*. This is crucial to the discipline of history.	The idea of an historian as detective is common. This activity relates to the child - one day they will be history and are part of the pageant of the past. Why not bury a time capsule in the school ground - 'Life in our School' - the children being responsible for the contents.	AT 3/4 S & C

Celts Unit

Title	Purpose	Focus/Information/Extensions	AT & PESC
Celtic Homes	To examine the interdependence of roles within the village and the hierarchy of the tribe. To look at different house building styles from the period.	House building was dependent on local materials. Stress differences in building styles. Focal point of the community geared to existence. Technology was sophisticated.	AT 3/4 S & C
Celtic Craftsmen	To identify artefacts and appreciate skills and artistry of craftsmen. Speculation, reasoned argument.	Helmet made of bronze. Bronze shield, probably ceremonial. Silver bowl used in religious ceremonies. Torc (neck ring) made of electrum (alloy of silver and gold), a symbol of authority. Bronze hand mirror. Group/paired work to be encouraged plus further research on the artefacts.	AT 2/3/4 C
Celtic Technology	To appreciate technology. A 'card' game. Interactive. Prioritising the changes to standards of living brought by use of iron.	Important to share results. Encourage research. There is obviously no 'right' answer but debates will promote speaking and listening skills.	AT 1/2/3/4 E, S & C
Lindow Man - A Mystery	To understand that this archaeological detective story has enhanced our knowledge of Iron Age man. To write creatively from known facts.	Focus on known facts - encourage oral responses first to the mystery. Share ideas. Additional research on costumes, names, settlements and religious ceremonies will enrich the writing.	AT 1/3/4 S
What did the Celts Look Like?	To think about Celtic appearance. What we know of the Celts appearance is dependent on the writings of the classical authors. They may of course be biased or exaggerated.	Resource material needs to be provided so that children can complete the ghost outlines. This activity could lead to interesting experimental work - recreating Celtic costume, investigating textiles and materials available to Celtic man.	AT 2/3/4 C
Boudicca's Revolt!	To understand that the Romans had a precarious grip on Britain in A.D. 61. To appreciate the cause and effect of the revolt and the charisma of a female leader.	Boadicea is a C17th spelling mistake. Rosemary Sutcliffe's 'Song For a Dark Queen' is a powerful source for this story. The Celtic numbers in the final battle hampered their movement - that and lack of discipline in battle. Roman military discipline won the day	AT 1/3/4 P
Celtic Art	To appreciate mathematical properties of art and the beauty of design.	Look for symmetry reflections. This is a late Celtic piece from one of the Gospels in the Book of Durrow. Look for other patterns on shields, jewellery, carvings, mirrors, etc.	AT 3 C
Four Seasons	To show that the Celtic seasons differed slightly to our own (especially in name). The organisation of the calendar was fundamental to the tribe's existence - link to farming.	Encourage individual response to illustration activity after oral discussion. Relate to today and especially local customs which are often rooted in Celtic pagan ritual.	AT 1/4 S & C

© 1990 Folens Limited

Title	Purpose	Focus/Information/Extensions	AT & PESC
Hill Fort	The concept of defence should be stressed - also the continual inter-tribal rivalry and warfare.	Strong line to drama - create your own hill fort community - let children be responsible for deciding roles and positions of features. Best of all, visit one near your school if possible.	AT 3/4 E & C
Figures in the Landscape	To arouse curiosity and knowledge of these figures and to promote a creative writing activity based on imaginative reconstruction.	Teachers may not want to discuss the symbolism of that other famous figure 'The Cerne Abbas Giant'! Research sizes and speculate why they might have been made. Try screen printing or stencil pictures. Create some music to go with the pictures and writing the children have produced.	AT 1/2/3/4 S & C

Romans Unit

Title	Purpose	Focus/Information/Extensions	AT & PESC
Invasion Britain	To understand that the invasion of Britain took 3 attempts spanning 100 years.	The quotes are taken from classical writers - debate and reasoned argument should be encouraged. The picture might be exploited for its evidence of Roman invasion ships.	AT 1/2/3/4 P
Legionary	To understand the dress and equipment of a Roman legionary. To appreciate the function of equipment and weaponry.	Most soldiers serving in Britain were auxiliaries recruited from other parts of the empire. Only Romans could join the legions. Discuss marching 20 miles a day carrying weapons and armour, and a spade and 2 wooden stakes to make a stockade. A sleeping cloak, cooking pot, 2 spears, corn and dried peas and salt.	AT 3/4 P
Town Planner	To appreciate the deliberate sophistication of Roman town planning - compared with the haphazard building of other cultures.	Look for Roman towns on O.S. maps - especially those with Roman endings, e.g. 'eter' - as in Exeter, cestra, caestra, etc. The public buildings, town houses, shops, baths, etc, need further study.	AT1/3/4 E, S & C
Roman Villa	The concept of 'landed gentry' - rich Roman landlords. Country estates, self-sufficiency and market economy.	Visit a Roman villa if possible. It will be necessary to research further, a typical day around a villa. Also, opportunities to investigate furniture and interior decoration. Estate agent details would be useful to help children with 'jargon'.	AT 1/3/4 E,S & C
Roman Roads	To understand the Roman road network in terms of civil engineering and as a communication network.	Many routes still exist - can children find them on a modern road map? Reference material will need to be found for translation into Roman names for towns.	AT 1/2/3 E
Curses!	To appreciate in a simple way, the Romans' fascination for good luck charms and their gods.	Encourage creativity based on children's experiences. Displayed, the children would find it fun to read each others' work.	AT 2/4 S & C
A Roman Wall Painting	Using a real Roman wall painting from Pompeii to discover dress, hairstyle, etc.	The idea is for the children to act as 'wall plaster painters' and to create appropriate colour schemes and look more closely at facial expression in painting. He was a lawyer. The stylus and wax tablet tell us that she was literate and therefore upper class Roman.	AT 1/2 C

© 1990 Folens Limited

Title	Purpose	Focus/Information/Extensions	AT & PESC
Saxons Unit			
Sea Wolves!	To empathise with the fear and terror the Saxon raiders would have instilled upon a population unprotected by the retreating Roman Legions.	A creative writing activity. The imagery of the ships' prow is powerful. Discuss thoughts, feelings and outcomes before children begin writing.	AT 1/2/4 P
Sutton Hoo: Part 1	To look at the greatest archaeological discovery this century - The Sutton Hoo ship burial.	This activity focuses on the ship itself. It should be stressed that only marks stained into the sand remained - it draws on the epic poem Beowulf.	AT 1/2/3/4 E, S & C
Sutton Hoo: Part 2	Looking at burial customs of the Saxons. Pagan. Thought to be the grave of Raedwald: an East Anglian king.	The treasures (the grave goods) are truly remarkable and should be discussed fully. Children should speculate as to whether they think there was a body or not. This activity could be compared with the first activity in the book.	AT 1/2/3/4 E, S & C
Saxon and Viking Writing	To understand that the Vikings and Saxons possessed a peculiar alphabet style - different from our own.	Note - no loops or tails in this alphabet. This allowed easy carving on stone, wood, ivory, etc. Look for other examples. The alphabets prove the close link between these 2 cultures.	AT 2/4 E & C
Anglo Saxon Riddles	To appreciate the literary heritage of the Saxon period.	A creative language activity based upon historical literature. It's not difficult to find other sources which should be read to the children. Children should be encouraged to read their riddles aloud - as the Saxons did!	AT3 C
Life in an Anglo Saxon Village	To stress the almost slum/ghetto style of building - knowledge is based on archaeological evidence.	A comparison activity between Saxon times and today. Out of these conditions were made some of the most exquisite jewellery and artefacts - the Dark Ages?	AT 1/3/4 S
Don't Burn the Cakes!	To understand that King Alfred's reign provided reforms that still exist today. 'Danelaw' concept should be clearly stated.	The story of Alfred 'burning the cakes' might be told. Children are asked for opinions and to prioritise facts. The debates and oral explanations should be explored fully.	AT 1/2/3/4 P
The Last Anglo Saxon King: 1042 - 1066	To refer to three types of evidence for our knowledge about Edward. His death brought about the invasion - cause and effect.	Children will need to be shown where the three great kingdoms are. Stress Edward's Norman connections.	AT 1/2/3 P
Vikings Unit			
Viking Attack on Lindisfarne!	To investigate the first recorded attack by the Vikings.	Interpretation and response to two pieces of evidence relating directly to the first attack on Lindisfarne. Children will need to refer to maps to find out where this is.	AT 1/2/3/4 P
Viking Ship	To understand that the Vikings had a rich literary tradition. The Kenning was a distinctive poetic form.	A collection of ideas from the class might be a way of introducing this activity. Encourage collaborative work. Drafting is also important.	AT 3 C
Traders and Craftsmen	To identify and explain some Viking artefacts. (All from York Coppergate dig.)	Children are asked to be 'experts' - good opportunity for drama, they take on role of expert. The teacher takes on role of exhibition organiser. The 'experts' tell the teacher about the exhibits!	AT 2/3/4 E & C

© 1990 Folens Limited

Title	Purpose	Focus/Information/Extensions	AT & PESC
The Viking World	To appreciate and understand the extent of the Viking world. Seamanship was vital to exploration.	The courageousness of the Vikings should not be underestimated. Homelands should be stressed. Good opportunities for graphicacy work. Which parts of the world were they ignorant of?	AT 1/4 E
Viking Dress	To discover what the Vikings looked like based upon archaeological evidence.	Focus is upon the sources by which we know about Viking dress. Comparisons might be made with costume today or the other cultures studied. Materials and tailoring could be investigated.	AT 2/3 C
Your Move Snarri!	To play a typical Viking board game of attack and defence - strategy is all important. The game is based upon archaeological evidence.	Children could make their own Viking games. The attackers can only stop the Hnefi escaping by manoeuvring the pieces in parallel with the defenders - see if the children can discover this.	AT 3 C
Ship Shapes	To understand the magnificent maritime heritage of the Vikings. Archaeological evidence is vital to this activity.	Different ships for different purposes should be discussed. Try chalking the dimensions on the playground to appreciate sizes and shapes. Look at Bayeux Tapestry for shipbuilding scenes.	AT 2/3/4 E
Viking Homes	To compare Viking homes with the children's own. To appreciate that building style is dependent upon local building resources.	Comparing and contrasting living styles will prove the differences between our culture and the Vikings. How might future generations look back on our so called civilised/technological society?	AT 1/3 S
A Viking Feast	To consider what the Vikings ate - a question we might ask of all cultures. Archaeological evidence at York has provided us with a wealth of understanding.	Try speculating what else the Vikings *might* have eaten. Why not prepare a Viking feast based upon the evidence here. Fragments of food glued onto cards could also be used to give children the experience of working in the manner of an archaeologist.	AT 2/3/4 S
Viking Picture Stones	To examine an artistic tradition taken from the Saxon art. In comparison with other art forms, it is quite primitive.	Other examples of picture stones should be found and discussed. Why not try carving in plaster and painting?	AT 2/4 S & C

Normans Unit

Title	Purpose	Focus/Information/Extensions	AT & PESC
Countdown to Invasion 1066.....	The three units that complete the book focus on the Norman Invasion. The best source of course is the Bayeux Tapestry (really an embroidery). Children should be aware of the causes and the consequences of the invasion and the principal characters involved in the story.	A magnificent story beautifully told through the embroidery. Children should be encouraged to decide who had most claim to the throne. Opportunities for oral work. Focus on *one* episode from the tapestry.	AT 1/2/3/4 P & S & C
Invasion 1066!		The geographical element in the story is important. The Saxon army - especially the elite housecarls - marched over 600 miles and fought two major battles in a matter of weeks. The weather also plays its part.	
Saxon versus Norman: Hastings 1066		The Bayeux embroidery provides evidence of uniforms - and how the battle was fought. Try embroidering *one* character in wool on hessian - it encourages observation and appreciation of the whole tapestry.	

© 1990 Folens Limited

How do we Know?

The people you will meet in these activities were the people who invaded, settled, lived and died in Britain up to 2 000 years ago.

Most of what we know about these people - how and where they lived - has been discovered by **archaeologists**.

There is a problem. Archaeologists only find **fragments** of the past - they will never know the complete truth. Therefore, they must look at the **clues** and make a best guess from the **evidence** that they find.

✎ Draw a picture of yourself in this space, as you look today. If you wish, fix a photograph to the space. Show yourself wearing your favourite clothes.

✎ If you died what favourite possessions would you like buried with you?

_____
_____
_____
_____

✎ If archaeologists were to discover you in 2 000 years' time what changes would have taken place?

_____
_____
_____

What would have rotted away?

_____
_____

What would have remained intact?

_____
_____

What could archaeologists tell from the remains about your life?

_____
_____

Celtic Homes

At Buster in Hampshire an Iron Age 'roundhouse' was reconstructed by archaeologists to discover how the Celts built their houses.

In Cornwall, another kind of building was found.
This building is called a 'courtyard' house because all the rooms of the dwelling open out onto a central courtyard.

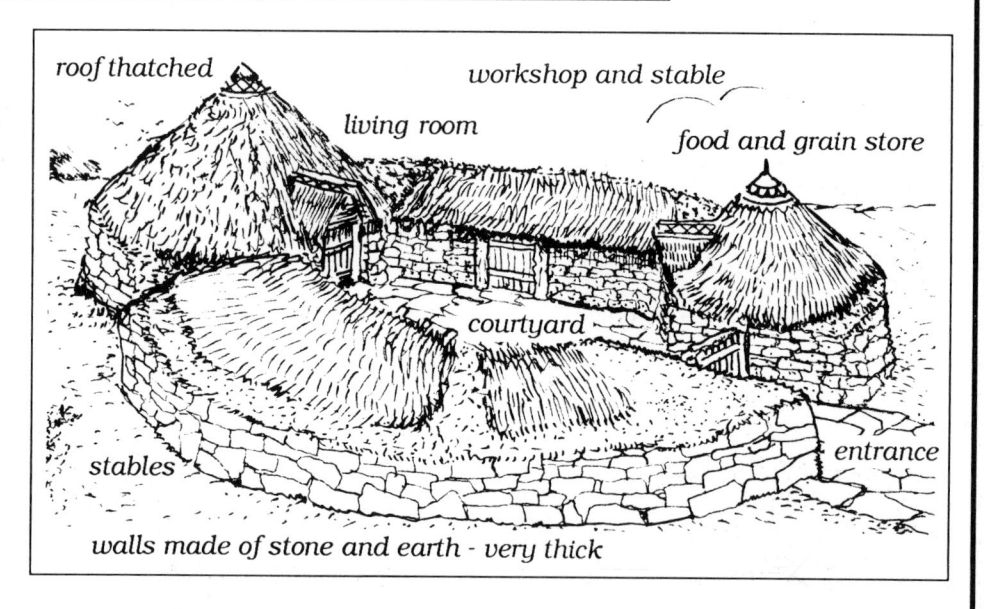

Labels on diagram: roof thatched, workshop and stable, living room, food and grain store, courtyard, stables, entrance, walls made of stone and earth - very thick

✏️ Tick the words in this list that best describe the living conditions in an iron age village.

healthy	clean	hygienic	pleasant
comfortable	safe	uncomfortable	smelly
cold	unhealthy	damp	exciting
draughty	difficult	dingy	convenient
warm	boring	stuffy	

✏️ These people were self-sufficient. This means that everything they needed they had to make, grow or gather from nature.

What would have provided them with:
- meat?
- bread?
- milk?
- eggs?
- sweetening?
- flour?

What would they have used to make:
- clothes?
- shoes?
- needles?
- tools?
- buckets?

© 1990 Folens Limited   This page may be photocopied for classroom use only

Celtic Craftsmen

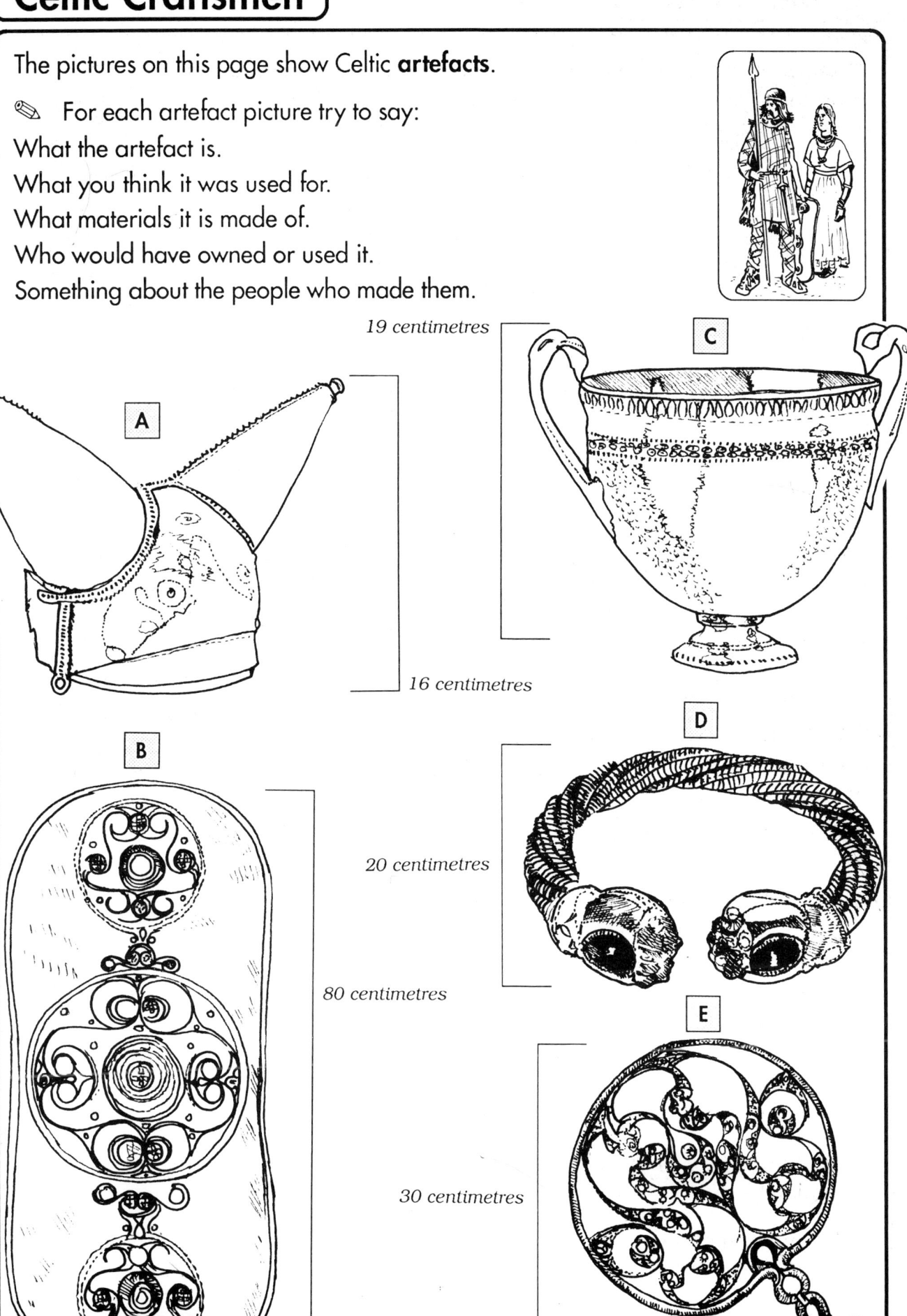

The pictures on this page show Celtic **artefacts**.

✏️ For each artefact picture try to say:

What the artefact is.
What you think it was used for.
What materials it is made of.
Who would have owned or used it.
Something about the people who made them.

A

19 centimetres

C

16 centimetres

B

20 centimetres

D

80 centimetres

E

30 centimetres

© 1990 Folens Limited   This page may be photocopied for classroom use only

Celtic Technology

The Celtic people who **migrated** to Britain 700 years before Christ was born brought with them the ability to work with iron - so the name given to this period is the Iron Age! Being able to work with iron brought an improved way of life for the people.

■ Below are seven statement cards.
Discuss with your partner, or in a small group, which of the statements are the *most* important. Try to decide which order they should go in, from 1 to 7.

a Iron swords and spear heads were better weapons - important for defending against raiders.

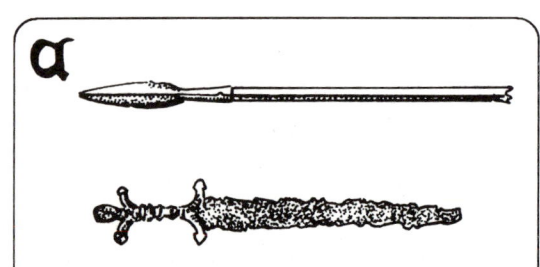

b Domestic items - knives, chains, pots and pans, fire irons and ladles all improved the standard of living.

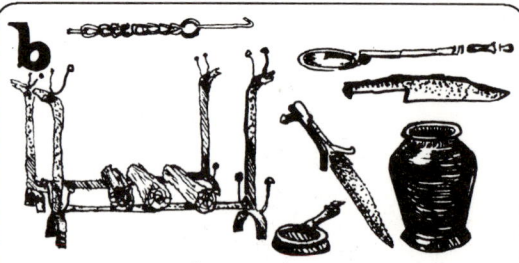

c Iron shears meant that sheep's fleeces could be cut more easily. Iron pins allowed woollen and flax materials to be sewn better. Cloth could be cut more accurately which meant better fitting clothes.

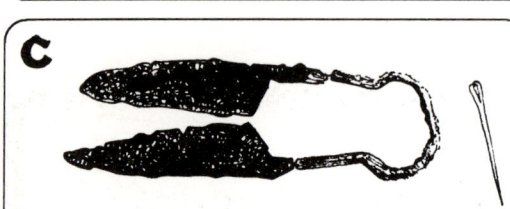

d Cooking pots made of iron lasted longer and could be put directly over a fire.

e 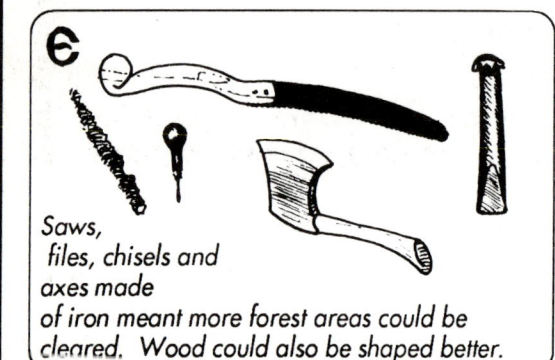 Saws, files, chisels and axes made of iron meant more forest areas could be cleared. Wood could also be shaped better.

f Chariots were important to the Celts, especially in battle. Iron rims for the wheels meant that they lasted longer and were faster.

g Scythes, ploughs and other farming tools lasted longer and meant that the ground could be worked more easily. More food could therefore be harvested.

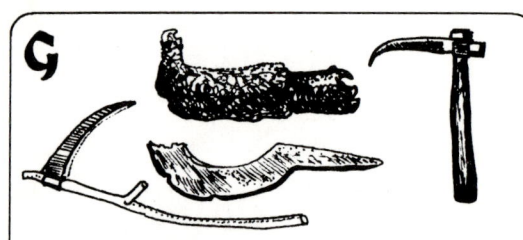

✂ Cut these cards out and paste them in the order you decide upon.

✎ By the side of each one write out your reasons for ordering them in the way you did.

Lindow Man - A Mystery

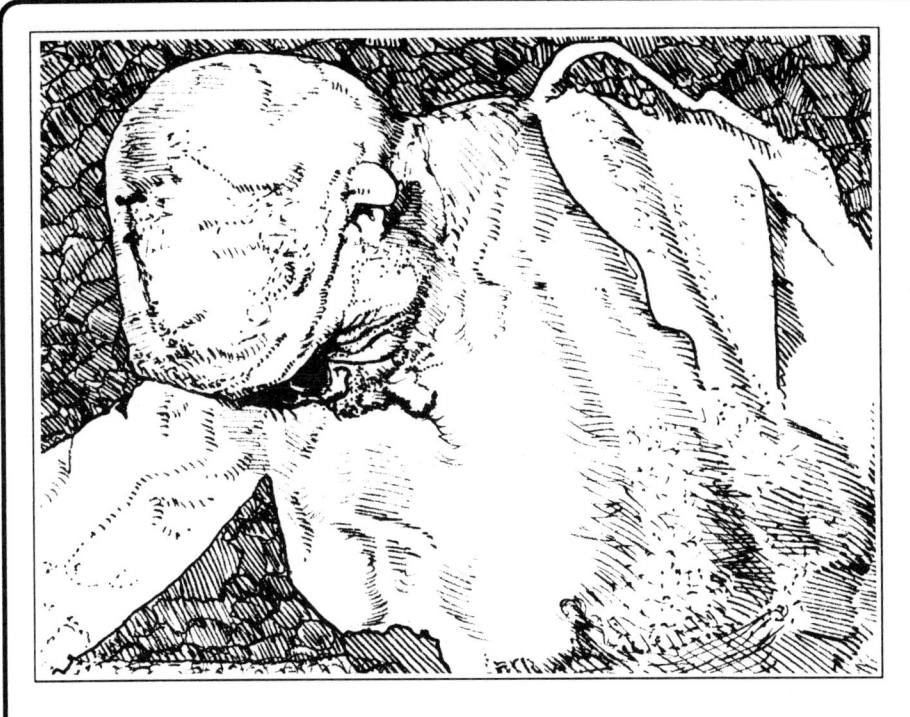

Digging for peat in Lindow Marsh in Cheshire some workmen accidentally came across half a body ..... The police and archaeologists were brought in to try and solve the mystery. They discovered that the man had died over 2 000 years ago but the peat had preserved the body .....

But how did he die?

Facts! The archaeologists have discovered that .....
1. Lindow Man had ginger hair, a moustache and beard which was neatly trimmed.
2. His finger nails were neatly cut suggesting that he did not do rough work.
3. He was strangled with a cord which was knotted. His neck was broken.
4. He was hit on the head which fractured the skull.
5. He was pushed or fell face forward into a pool of water.
6. He was naked apart from a fox fur band around his arm.
7. His last meal was probably barley cakes (partly burnt) and a porridge mixture.

✎ Reconstruct the last hours of Lindow Man.

Give him a real name and try and imagine how he might have felt on his last day alive.

_____
_____
_____
_____
_____
_____

What did the Celts Look Like?

✎ Use the descriptions on this page to help you complete these outlines of a Celtic man and woman.

Cloaks were often worn.

Men's hair was often stiffened into spikes and scraped back like a horse's mane.

The Celts were great show offs! Their clothes were brightly coloured and chequered like tartan.

Neck rings were worn and bronze pins fastened clothes together.

Warriors favoured swords and spears as favourite weapons. Shields were made of layers of wood and leather.

Around their necks they wore twisted cords of metal called torcs.

They wore moustaches which acted like a strainer when they drank.

Their hair was often worn in long plaits.

Women wore leather shoes.

Women wore floor length skirts.

© 1990 Folens Limited   This page may be photocopied for classroom use only

Boudicca's Revolt!

> "She was very tall, the glance of her eye most fierce; her voice harsh. A great mass of the reddish hair fell down to her hips. Around her neck was a large golden necklace, and she always wore a tunic of many colours over which she fastened a thick cloak with a broach. Her appearance was terrifying ....."
>
> Dio Cassius
> *Roman History*

AD 61: The Story

A Prasutagus, King of the Iceni tribe died, leaving half of his wealth to the Romans and half to his wife, Boudicca and their two daughters. ..... but Roman tax collectors looted his lands, whipped his wife and assaulted his daughters.

B The Iceni revolted! The Catuvellauni joined them.

C The Trinovantes joined the Iceni because the Romans had built a temple in their tribal capital.

D On the way to Colchester the Celtic tribes, led by Boudicca destroyed Roman villas and slaughtered the occupants.

E The Celts destroyed Colchester.

F The Romans had a problem. The nearest legions were in Lincoln, Gloucester and Wales. The 9th Legion marched from Lincoln, but was destroyed by the Celts.

G Seutonius, the Roman Governor was in Anglesey fighting the druids. When he heard the news that Britain was in revolt he marched towards London.

H London was a trading centre. Seutonius could not defend it and abandoned it. Boudicca destroyed London - deaths are estimated at 70 000.

I Boudicca decided to follow Seutonius and deal a final blow and force the Romans to leave Britain for good. Archaeologists do not know where the final battle took place - somewhere along Watling Street.

J The Romans had 10 000 men. Boudicca had many times that number. In the final battle 80 000 Britons were killed. The Romans lost 400 dead. It is said that Boudicca poisoned herself.

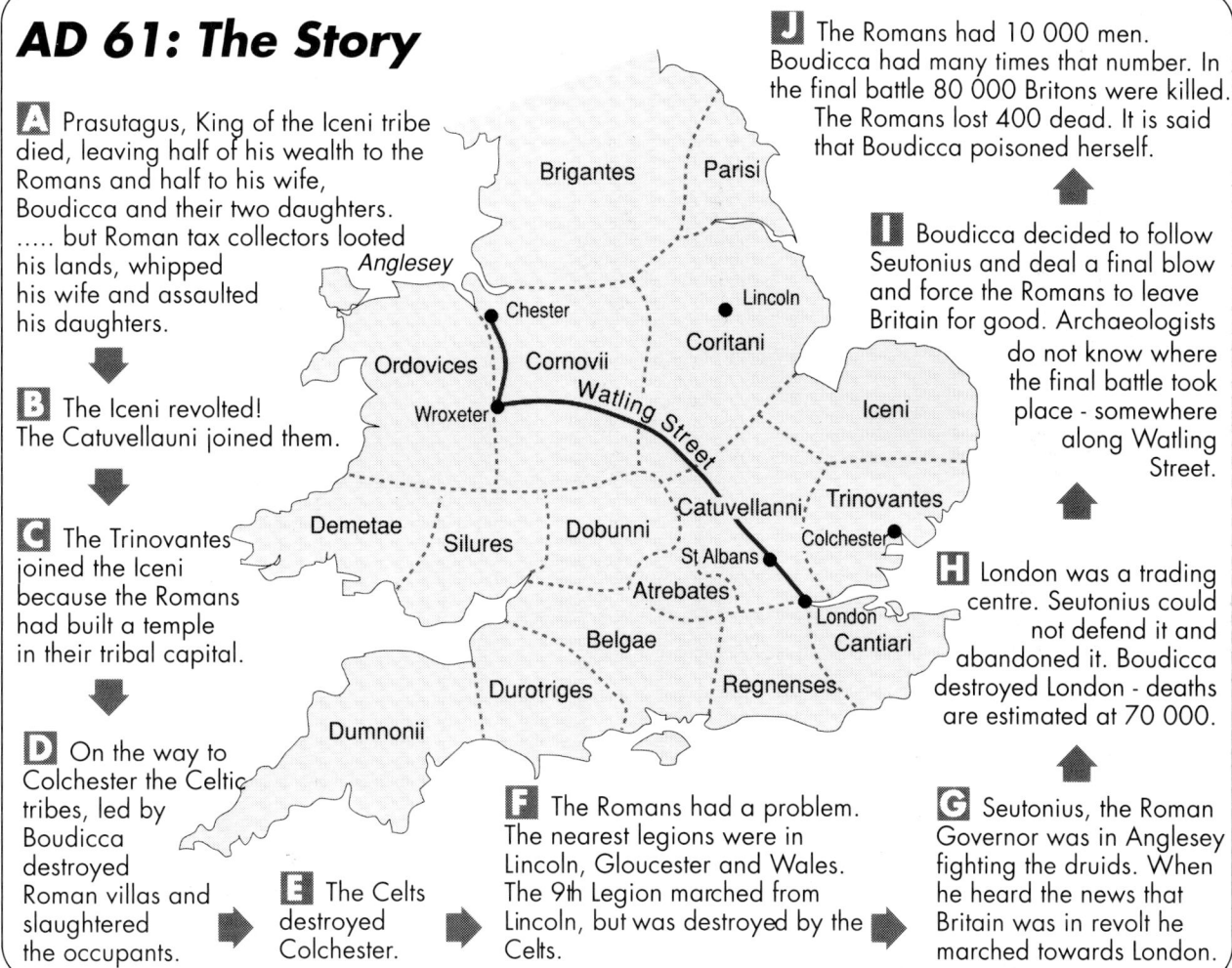

✏ Use the maps and the words on this page to tell the story of Boudicca's Revolt. Perhaps you could turn it into a tape recorded documentary!

Why do you think the Romans won the final battle?

What would have happened if Boudicca and the Celtic tribes had won the battle?

What would you do if you were Seutonius having won the battle?

The Final Battle

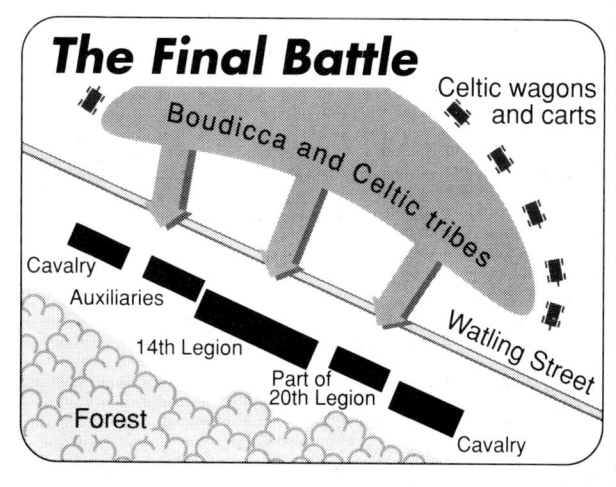

© 1990 Folens Limited   This page may be photocopied for classroom use only   15

Celtic Art

This is a drawing of a decorative medallion with interesting ribbons and four inscribed discs. It comes from the Gospel of St. John in the Book of Durrow.

✏️ As you can see part of the medallion is missing - can you complete it?
Will a mirror help you?
Try following the route of one or more of the ribbons using a coloured pencil.

Four Seasons

The four seasons of the Celtic year took place at important times for farmers. Good crops and healthy animals were vital for the tribe's survival. The ceremonies were held at the tribe's sacred places and were accompanied by feasting and dancing. Sacrifice to the gods was also a part of the ceremony.

✎ Make drawings in the spaces below to show the four seasons.

samhain (pronounced sov-ain)

October 31st

This marks the beginning of the Celtic year. It was a time when the Celts believed spirits stalked the land and darkness reigned. It was the most important festival.

Named after the god Lugh. A harvest festival celebration marked by the inventing of plays watched by the tribe.

Lughnasa (pronounced loo-nasa)

August 1st

Imbolg

February 1st

This late winter festival celebrated lambing time and that the ewes were producing milk. It also celebrated the goddess Brigid (pronounce Bree-itch) who was associated with oak trees (sacred to the Celts) and fire.

This marked the beginning of Summer for the Celts. It celebrates the god Belenos who encouraged the growth of crops and the health of cattle. Bonfires were lit and the cattle driven through the flames to purify them. The Druids (priests) made sacrifices so that the gods would give them a fruitful year.

Bealtine

May 1st

Research: What can you find out about the seasons and festivals of our calender? How are they different?

Hill Fort

The Celts defended themselves by building settlements on the tops of hills. In Great Britain, there are over 3 000 hill forts! Is there one near where you live?

✎ Suggest 3 reasons why it was a good idea to build a settlement on top of a hill.

1 _____
2 _____
3 _____

Look at the picture below of Maiden Castle in Dorset. It is probably the most famous Iron Age hill fort! Forts like this one were built by hand!
Even though it looks as though no one could capture it, the Romans did in 43 A.D.

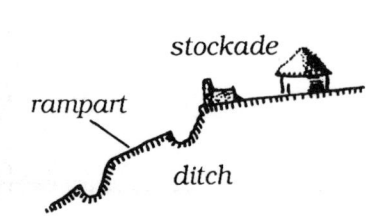

rampart *stockade* *ditch*

The entrances were the most vulnerable part of the fort and they were very carefully thought out.

■ Can you spot the entrances to Maiden Castle?
How many ditches does Maiden castle have?

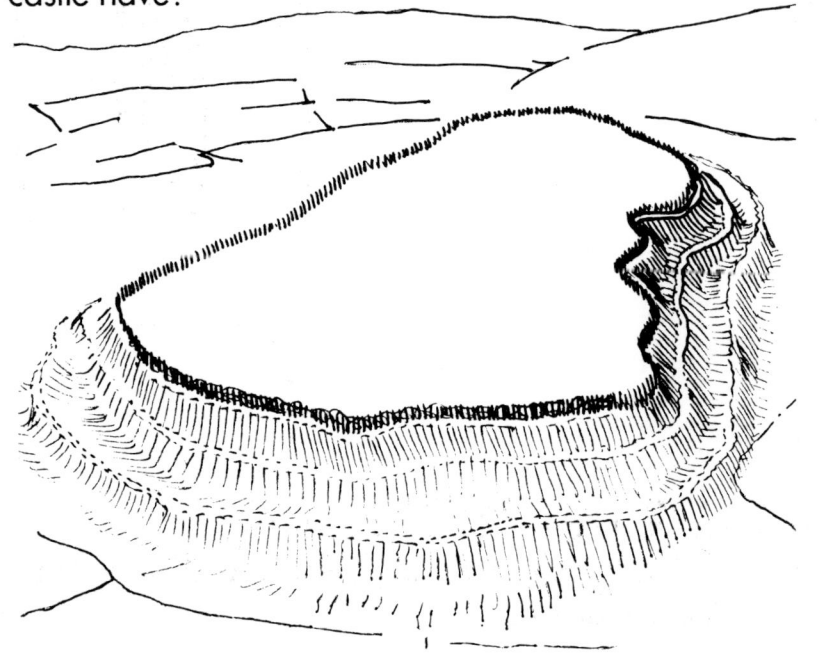

You are chief of a local tribe and decide to build a hill fort to protect your people.

✎ On the drawing, mark where you would put these things:
▼ the huts your people will live in
▼ the well
▼ piles of slingstones (in preparation for an attack)
▼ storage pits
▼ the blacksmith's forge
▼ horses and cattle
▼ entrance gates

© 1990 Folens Limited   This page may be photocopied for classroom use only

Figures in the Landscape

The Celts were responsible for creating strange figures in the landscape. In chalkland areas they cut away the turf to reveal the white chalk so that these incredible figures could be seen from afar.

Two of the most well known figures are the White Horse of Uffington and the Long Man of Wilmington in Sussex.

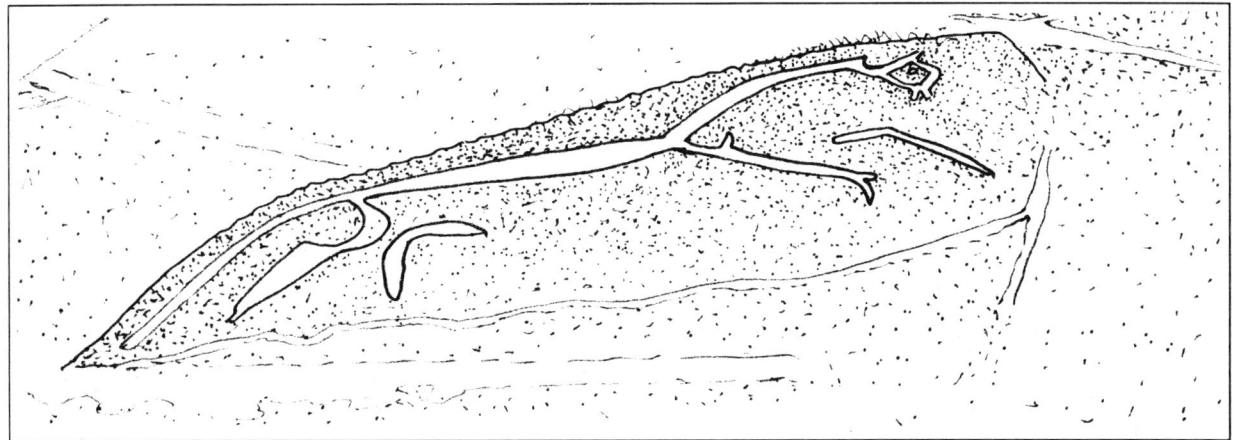

Horses were very special to the Celts. Epona was a horse goddess who also appears on Celtic coins.

✎ Create your own story about why the figures were made.

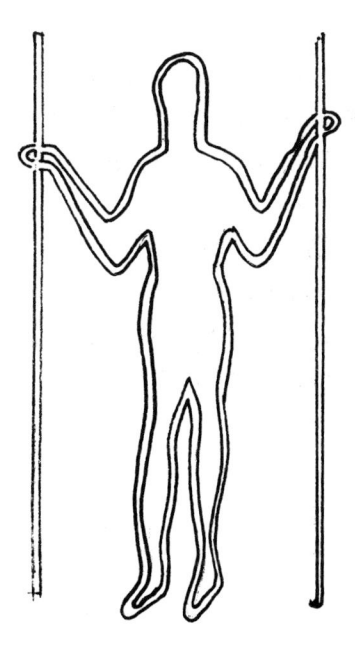

_____
_____
_____
_____
_____

_____
_____
_____

What kind of music would go well with your story?
Perhaps you could create your own landscape figure using white paint or chalk on the playground.

Invasion Britain

In 55 B.C. Julius Caesar, a Roman, invaded Britain for the first time. His small army could not defeat the Celtic tribes and he decided to return to France. The following year he returned with a much bigger army. Although he defeated a number of tribes he could not conquer the country. No more Romans came for nearly 100 years.

It is now the year 43 A.D.

The Emperor Claudius in Rome is deciding if he should invade Britain for a third time and make it a part of the Roman Empire. He gathers his scholars and councillors around him .....

✎ Read the following and prepare your advice to the Emperor. What will you advise him to do?

- The country of Britain is rich in slaves, furs and hunting dogs.
- The strength of the Britons lies in their infantry. Some also fight from chariots.
- 3 legions will be needed to guard the country because of the warlike tribes. Only 1 legion is needed to guard the whole of North Africa.
- The climate is wretched with its rain and mists but there is no extreme cold.
- We are dealing with barbarians. There is no great difference in the language spoken by the tribes.
- The soil will produce good crops but will not grow olives and vines.
- The country is wealthy in coal, salt, tin, pottery and marble.

Legionary

A Roman legionary was expected to march 20 miles a day with full equipment. He carried 2 wooden stakes and a spade to help protect himself by building a stockade. He carried his rations of corn and dried beans. As well as his sword and shield, he also carried 2 spears. They were designed to bend on impact so that they could not be thrown back by the enemy.

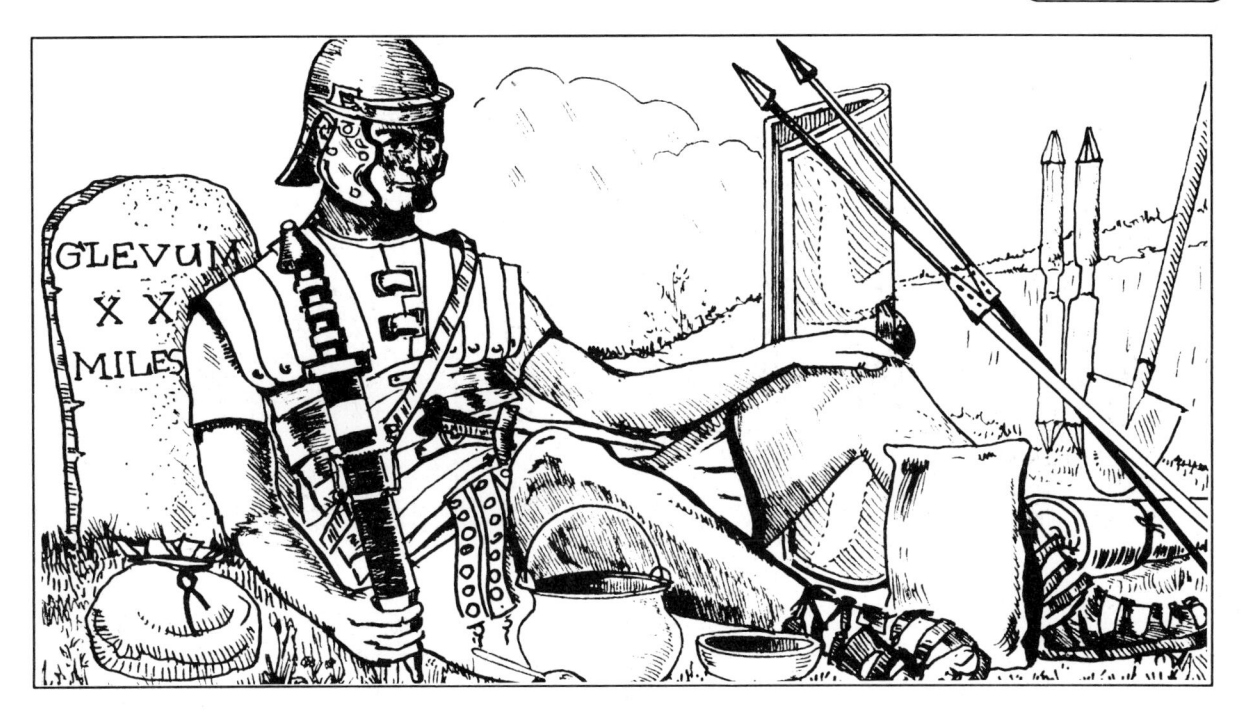

A new recruit writes to his mother back in Rome .....

Dearest Mother,
 I have arrived in Britain. The weather is miserable and we look forward to reaching our barracks at Glevum. I am very proud to be serving with the legion and want to tell you about my new uniform and equipment they have given me .....

© 1990 Folens Limited   This page may be photocopied for classroom use only

Town Planner

The Romans built dozens of towns in Britain although they were much smaller than our towns today. The towns were built on a grid pattern of streets. The buildings were laid out in blocks surrounded by gardens, orchards and parks. Not every block was built upon. The town was surrounded by a high stone wall.

You are a Roman town planner .....

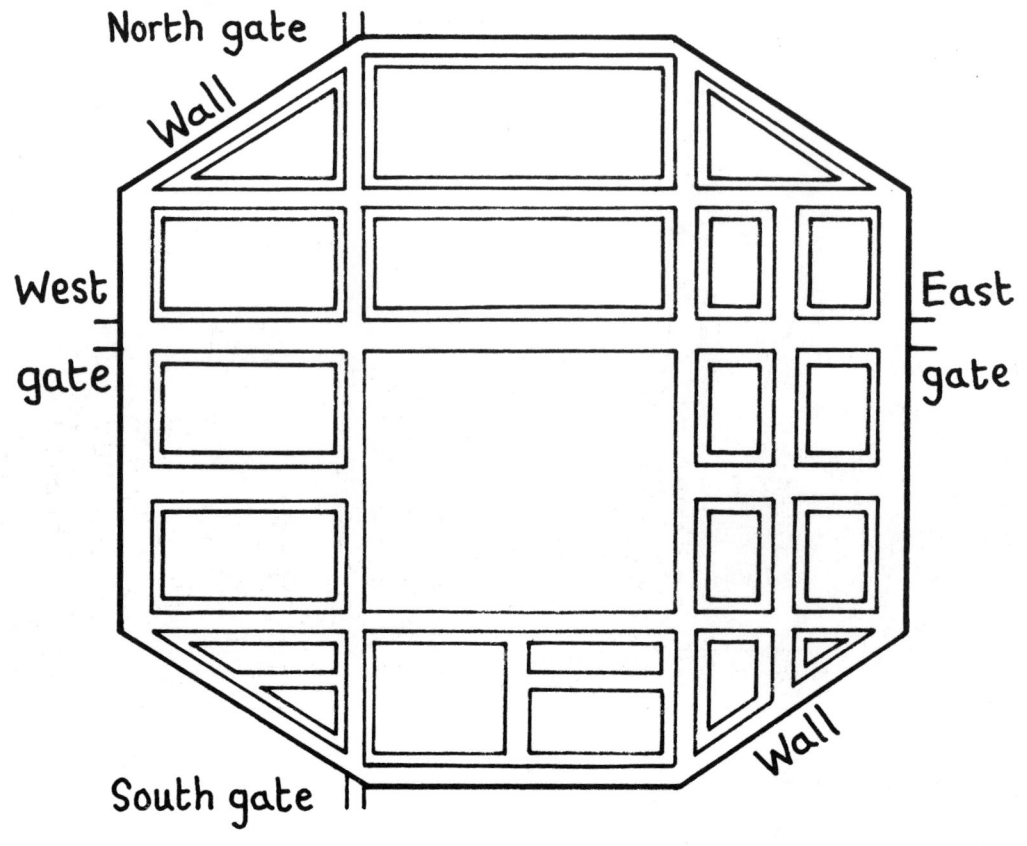

■ Decide where you will draw the blocks on your town plan above. The people who will live in this town will need all the modern conveniences of town life in Roman Britain.

✎ Where will you decide to build:
- ▼ The Forum (the main town square with a market place for shops, the law courts, the Town Hall and perhaps a temple).
- ▼ The baths.
- ▼ Other shops - food, clothes, tools, ornaments, pots, wine.
- ▼ Other temples.
- ▼ Inns.
- ▼ The town houses of the rich.
- ▼ The poor people's houses (often very close together).
- ▼ The theatre.
- ▼ Workshop.

Roman Villa

This picture is of a famous Roman Villa in Gloucestershire called Chedworth. Villas were country houses built on rich farmland. They were often elaborate buildings with many bedrooms, dining rooms, baths, gardens, courtyards and shrines. A family could show off its wealth by the rich furnishings, mosaic floors, painted plaster walls and sculptures. Sometimes many slaves were needed to work the farm, in the fields and orchards. Rooms were also built for the slaves, store rooms, kitchens, workshops and stables for animals.

Labels on picture: reception rooms, shrine and spring, reception hall, baths, furnace rooms, baths, bedrooms, dining rooms, kitchen, W.C., gardens, farm buildings.

✎ Imagine you are a Roman estate agent. You have been asked to sell this Villa - how would you advertise it?

Roman Roads

The towns of Roman Britain were linked by a system of roads. They were very straight and built by the soldiers but repaired and paid for by the local tribes!

✎ On your map link the Roman towns by drawing in these roads:

1. Chester - Wroxeter - Caerleon.
2. Caerleon - Gloucester - Cirencester - Silchester - London.
3. Exeter - Dorchester - Silchester.
4. London - Dover.
5. London - Lincoln - York (label this ERMINE STREET).
6. London - Leicester - Wroxeter (label this WATLING STREET).
7. Cirencester - Leicester - Lincoln (label this FOSSE WAY).
8. Chester - York.
9. Chester - Carlisle.
10. York - Hadrian's Wall.
11. Caerleon - Bath - Silchester.

Research

Can you find out the Roman names for these towns?

Here's one to start you off - Gloucester = Glevum

Which is the nearest Roman road to your school?

Fact: There are over 11 900 kilometres of Roman roads in Britain!

© 1990 Folens Limited   This page may be photocopied for classroom use only

Curses!

Have you ever thrown a coin into a fountain and made a wish?

When archaeologists were digging out the fountain at Aquae Sulis (Bath) they discovered over 12 000 Roman coins .....

They also found curious pieces of lead with 'curse' messages scratched on which were then rolled or folded up and thrown into the water as offerings to the gods.

✎ Write a good luck charm or a curse on the tablet above.
Write in capital letters and if you write backwards it helps the magic!

One such tablet held a message from a lady called Saturnina to the god Mercury complaining that she has lost some linen cloth. She promised a third of its value to Mercury and a third to the god Silvanus if it is returned to her!

© 1990 Folens Limited   This page may be photocopied for classroom use only

A Roman Wall Painting

This is perhaps one of the most famous wall paintings at Pompeii. This piece of evidence reveals the fashions of Romans, their hairstyles, and that their houses must have been richly decorated. We know the man's name - Terentius Neo - and like his friends and neighbours he died in the great eruption of Vesuvius.

■ All paintings are posed. Try creating different expressions by moving your head. How would you show - sadness, peacefulness, anger, grace, happiness. (Pay attention to your eyes!)

✏ What adjectives would you choose to describe the Romans in this wall painting?

_____
_____
_____
_____

■ What colours will you choose to complete this painting?

✏ Make a colour chart like you find in Do-It-Yourself shops and make up names for your colours.
Remember: 'Legionary sandal brown' is better than just 'brown'. Use pencil crayons and try to blend the colours.

© 1990 Folens Limited   This page may be photocopied for classroom use only

Sea Wolves!

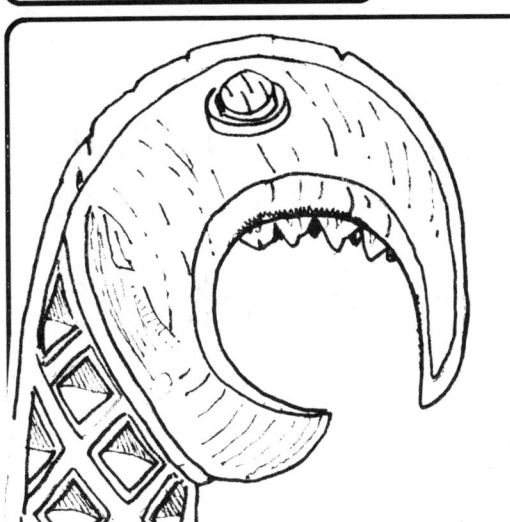

When Rome itself came under attack from the Goths it recalled the legions from the provinces. The message from Rome was 'defend yourself!' This left Britain, by now a wealthy, civilised country unprotected from the wrath of the Angles and Saxons from Denmark and Northern Germany.

✏ You are on the clifftop when you see Saxon pirate raiders heading straight for you. *Tell the story of what happens next .....*

_____
_____
_____
_____

Ship's prow of carved oak found in the river Scheldt, Belgium.

Sutton Hoo: Part 1

"Then the Geat Nation constructed for him a barrow on the headland - so high and broad that seafarers might see it from afar. They placed in the tomb brooches, rings, cups and jewels and all the trappings which they had plundered from the treasure hoard. They left the gold and treasure to the keeping of the earth, where yet it remains ....."

Beowulf

In 1939, the greatest British archaeological discovery was made near the river Deben in Suffolk. Here, there was a group of low circular burial mounds. Some had been robbed but the largest mound was excavated and inside was found a magnificent Anglo Saxon ship containing riches and wealth unknown to experts on the Saxons before .....

■ Look at this picture of the Anglo Saxon ship. Point out:
▼ excavation trenches
▼ the prow of the ship
▼ the ships plank's marks
▼ rivets that held the planks together
▼ cross frames
▼ central burial chamber

No wood or metal had survived, only stains in the sand leaving an outline of the ship.

In the Anglo Saxon poem 'Beowulf' we are given more clues:-

"The great sea bird rode over the breakers. And as soon as the Geats hoisted a sail, a bleached sea garment, the boat foamed at the prow and surged over the waves, urged on by the wind."

✎ Make a sketch showing what the ship might have looked like before it was buried.

© 1990 Folens Limited   This page may be photocopied for classroom use only

Sutton Hoo: Part 2

In the centre of the ship was a large chamber. Within it was set out a range of possessions that showed every aspect of the dead person's life. The archaeologists decided that this was a **pagan** burial (not Christian) and the objects would be needed by the dead person for their new life in 'the other world'.

Here is a list of some of the things that were found:

- spears
- iron stand

- shield
- 3 iron bound wooden buckets
- bronze bowl
- silver bowls

- spoons
- sword

- purse
- gold objects
- fragments of cloth

- an axe
- mail coat
- great silver dish
- pottery bottle
- iron lamp
- chains

- cauldrons
- a beaverskin bag

■ The archaeologists could not identify everything. Can you help them by identifying the artefacts shown in the pictures on this page?

✎ What sort of person do you think might own these objects. Tell the story of his burial in your own words .....

© 1990 Folens Limited   This page may be photocopied for classroom use only

Saxon and Viking Writing

Many objects belonging to the Saxons and Vikings had special marks called RUNES carved into stone, ivory, wood or metal. It was their alphabet. It is often called the 'FUTHORK' after the first letters of their alphabet.

Here is the complete Saxon runes list:

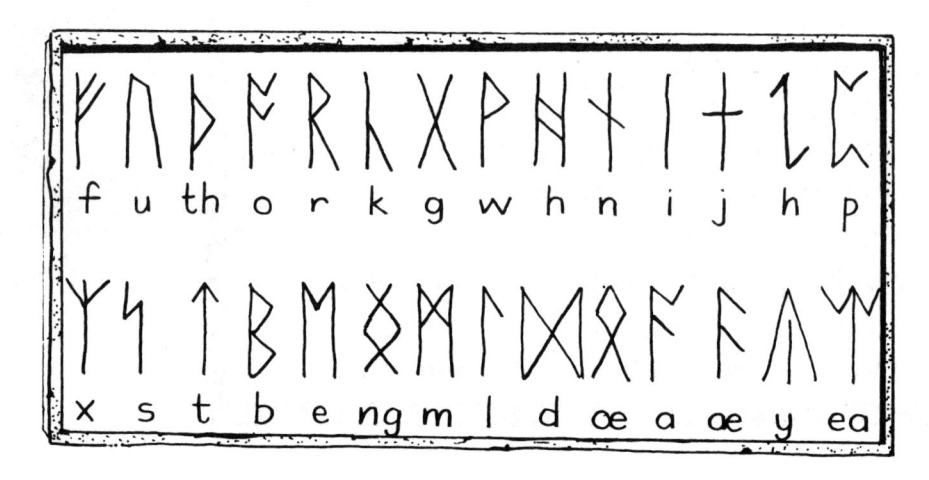

f u t h o r k g w h n i j h p
x s t b e ng m l d œ a œ y ea

Swords were precious objects to the Saxons - often they were marked with runes telling the owner's name or hiding a secret message.

✎ Write your name or message on this sword.

✎ Make up an advertising slogan for the Viking comb and case as though you were the craftsman.

The Viking alphabet was shorter with only 23 letters:

a b c d e f g h i k l m n o p q r s t u v w x y z

If a Saxon wrote to a Viking ..... could they understand each other?

Anglo Saxon Riddles

The Saxons were fond of riddles - guessing the identity of something which is disguised in a description.

Here is a translation of one - what do you think it is?

> The deep sea suckled me,
> The waves sounded over me.
> Rollers were my coverlet as I rested on my bed.
> I have no feet and frequently open my mouth to the flood.
> Sooner or later some man will consume me
> Who cares nothing for my shell.
> With the point of his knife he will pierce me through
> Ripping the skin away from my side
> And straight away eat me, uncooked, as I am .....

✎ Try writing one for yourself.
Here are some things you might like to create a riddle about:
- a sword
- a cooking pot
- a swan
- a ring
- a cloak

..... but it is better to think of one for yourself!

_____
_____
_____
_____
_____
_____
_____
_____

© 1990 Folens Limited   This page may be photocopied for classroom use only

Life in an Anglo Saxon Village

Saxon Times	How has life changed today?
Houses were densely packed together. Walls were made from planking or wattle fencing. Roofs were thatched. The houses were mainly rectangular. The houses would have been damp, dark and smoky. Windows, if there were any, did not have glass.	
Men's average height was 1.7 metres. Women's average height was 1.64 metres. Men lived to the age of 40 on average and women lived to 35 on average. 1 in 3 children died before the age of 10.	
The main diseases were: • chronic diarrhoea leading to malnutrition • physical stress from hard work led to arthritis, particularly of the spine • pregnancies were frequent and physically stressful - women died earlier than men	
The diet was limited. Meat: beef, pork, mutton and some poultry. Bread: made from either wheat, barley, oats or rye. Vegetables: carrots, beans, peas. Fruits: apple, pear, plum, raspberry, blackberry. Fish: shellfish, eel, trout, salmon, herring, mackerel.	
Rubbish was disposed of in deep pits (up to 3 metres deep) sealed with clay to stop the smells. When they were full they were dug out and spread on fields as fertiliser. Fresh water came from wells - the shaft was lined to stop it collapsing. Water was drawn from a bucket on the end of a rope.	
Tunics were commonly worn. Leather shoes covered feet. Pins to hold clothes together were made of bronze. Most cloth was of fine wool, woven on a loom and mainly coloured red, blue or yellow. People lived and slept in *one* set of clothes.	

Don't burn the Cakes!

Alfred was born in 849 and died in 899. He lived at a time when England was constantly at war with the Danes. During the 9th century England was divided among the four great independent Anglo Saxon Kingdoms: MERCIA, NORTHUMBRIA, EAST ANGLIA and WESSEX. So powerful were the Vikings that by 878 only Wessex remained ..... but .....

"The force stole in Midwinter, after twelfthnight, to Chippenham. They rode over Wessex and occupied it and drove many of the people over the sea. They overcame the rest except for King Alfred and a small party who retreated and hid in the Somerset marshes..."

The Anglo Saxon Chronicle

Alfred build his army again and defeated the Vikings led by Guthrum at a place called Ethandan. A peace treaty was arranged and Guthrum was even baptised a Christian.

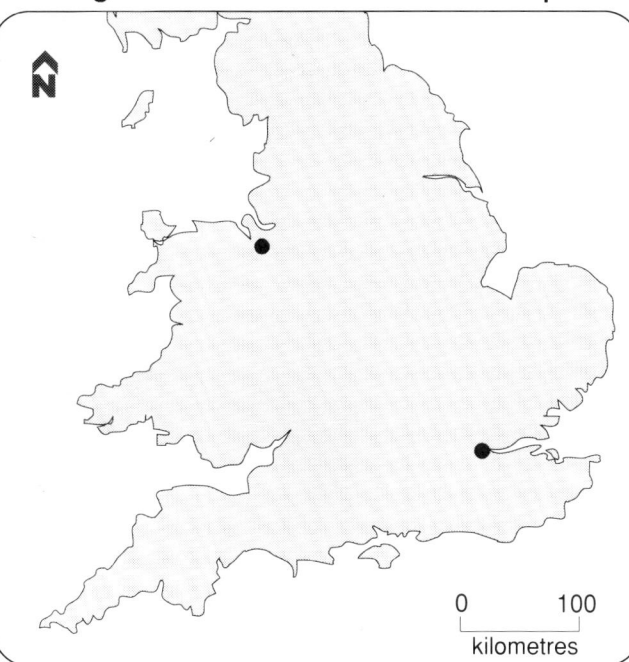

A silver penny showing King Alfred. How is this different from a modern penny?

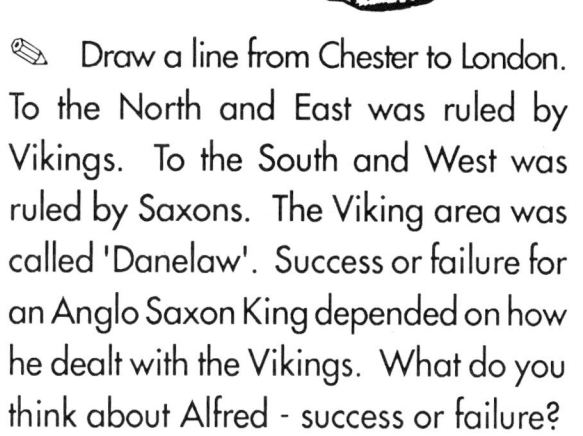

✎ Draw a line from Chester to London. To the North and East was ruled by Vikings. To the South and West was ruled by Saxons. The Viking area was called 'Danelaw'. Success or failure for an Anglo Saxon King depended on how he dealt with the Vikings. What do you think about Alfred - success or failure?

King Alfred was called 'The Great!' His achievements remain with us today.

He built England's first navy	
He united Britain against the Vikings	
He rewrote the laws of the land	
He improved the army	
He ordered bishops to translate the Latin books into English so more people could read	
He wanted more people to read and write and even set up a school in his royal palace	
He defended towns (called 'burhs') by building walls and ditches - the people felt safer	

✎ Which do you think are his most important achievements?
List them in order of importance - 1 = most important; 7 = least important.

© 1990 Folens Limited   This page may be photocopied for classroom use only

The Last Anglo Saxon King: 1042-1066

Edward the Confessor was the last Anglo-Saxon King. Two pieces of evidence show what he looked like:

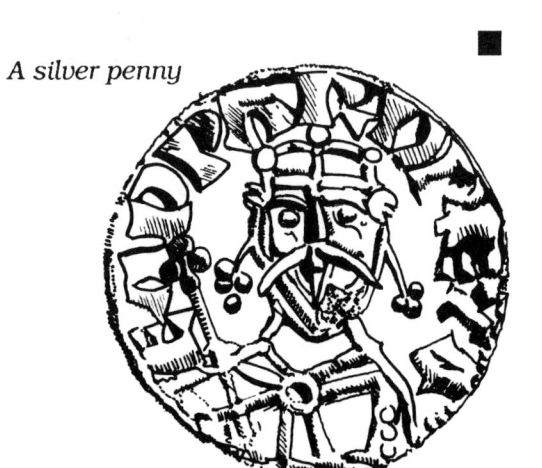

A silver penny

- Point out:
  - ▼ his crown
  - ▼ the six pearls dangling from his crown
  - ▼ his moustache
  - ▼ his mace

Before Edward became King of England he lived in Normandy in France. His mother, Emma, was the daughter of the Duke of Normandy. His father was the English king Ethelred the Unready.

He promised William, Duke of Normandy the crown of England when he died. Edward had no children of his own.

Britain at this time was divided into 3 great kingdoms, each one ruled by an earl.

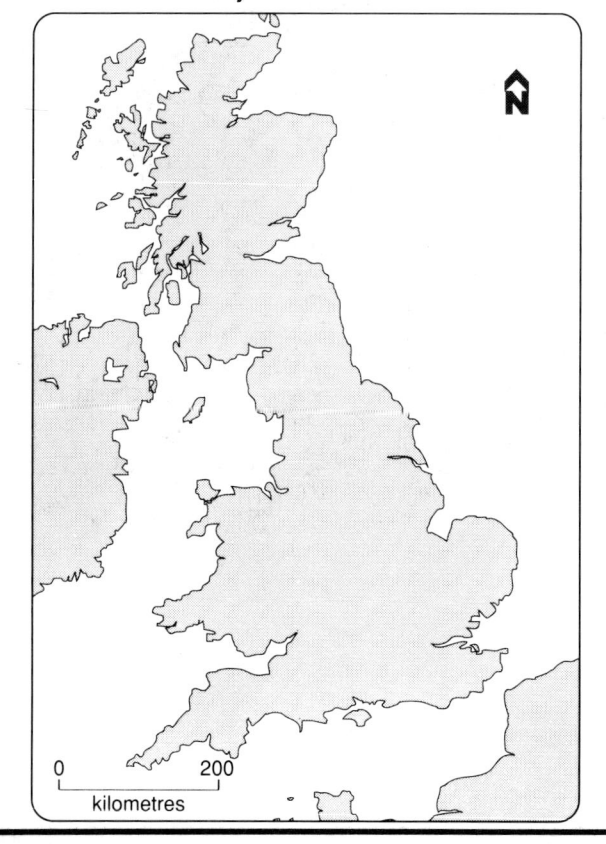

The Bayeux tapestry - really it is an embroidery.

✎ Which words best describe Edward? Put a circle around those you think appropriate.

elderly	proud
stupid	cowardly
stern	heroic
sad	intelligent

Research

Try to find out where the following places were:
The Kingdom of Wessex, ruled by Earl Harold.
The Kingdom of Mercia, ruled by Earl Edwin.
The Kingdom of Northumbria, ruled by Earl Morcar.
Mark them on the map.
Also mark in York, London and Hastings.

Viking Attack on Lindisfarne!

'In this year fierce, foreboding omens came over the land of Northumbria, and wretchedly terrified the people. There were excessive whirlwinds, lightning storms, and fiery dragons were seen flying in the sky. These signs were followed by great famine, and shortly after in the same year, on January 8th, the ravaging of the heathen men destroyed God's church at Lindisfarne through brutal robbery and slaughter.'

The Anglo Saxon Chronicle

✎ How might the Vikings have recorded the same story?

_____
_____
_____
_____
_____
_____

The entry in the Anglo Saxon Chronicle is one piece of written evidence. Among the ruins of the monastery was found this piece of evidence carved in stone.

✎ How would you describe the figures and what do you think the stone means?

_____
_____
_____
_____

Viking Ship

"Gold Mouthed splendid beasts of the mast, bright painted"

The Vikings used a technique in writing or storytelling called a 'KENNING'.

A Kenning was a description of something without using the real name. For example, the sea might be called 'the whale's road'.

The Vikings were great travellers and explorers by sea and river in their sleek ships which could be sailed or rowed.

✎ Try writing a Kenning about a Viking ship. Remember, after the title the words Viking Ship will not reappear.

Traders and Craftsmen

You are preparing some of the most recent finds from the archaeological dig at York for an exhibition.

✎ Write some words of explanation to go with each artefact.

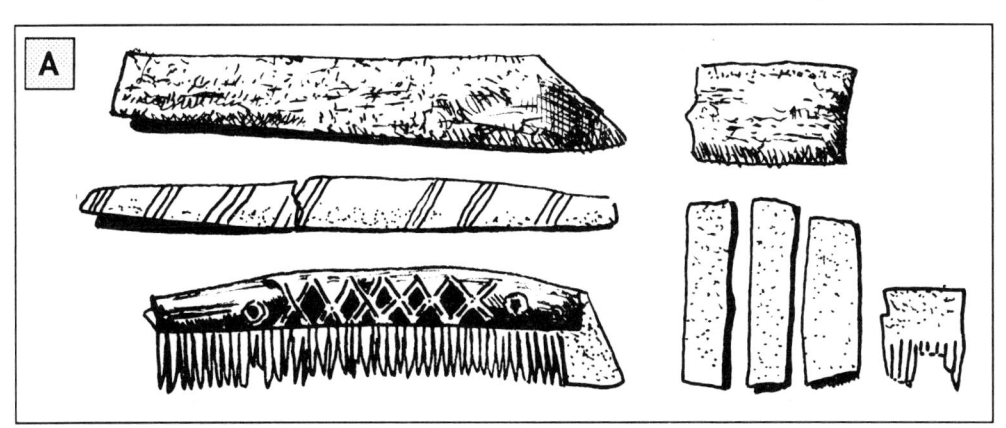

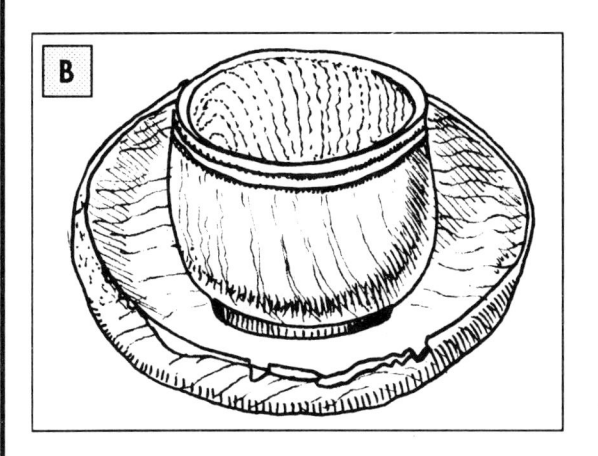

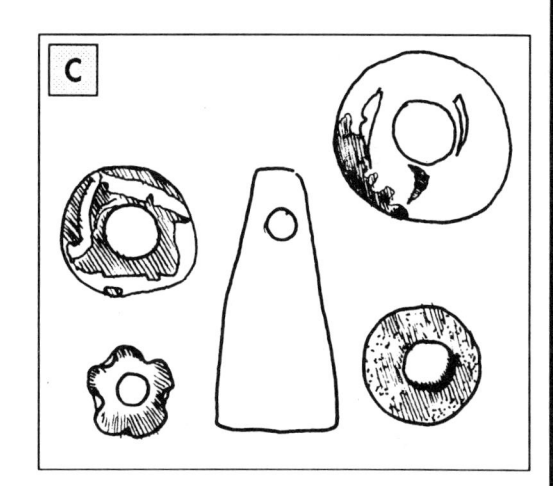

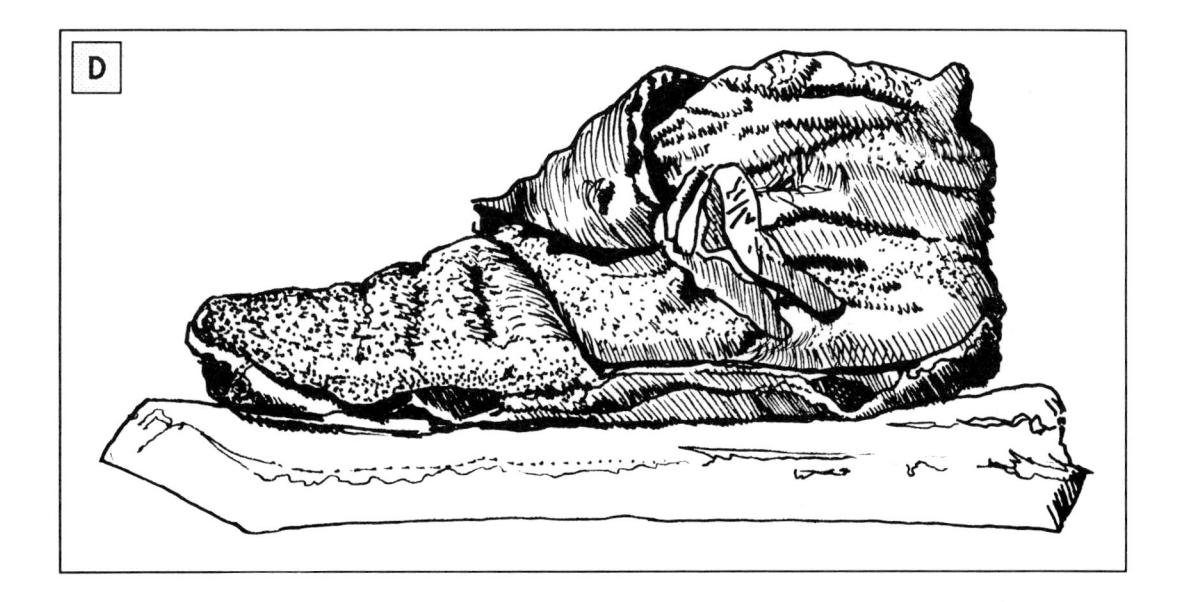

A

B

C

D

© 1990 Folens Limited   This page may be photocopied for classroom use only   37

The Viking World

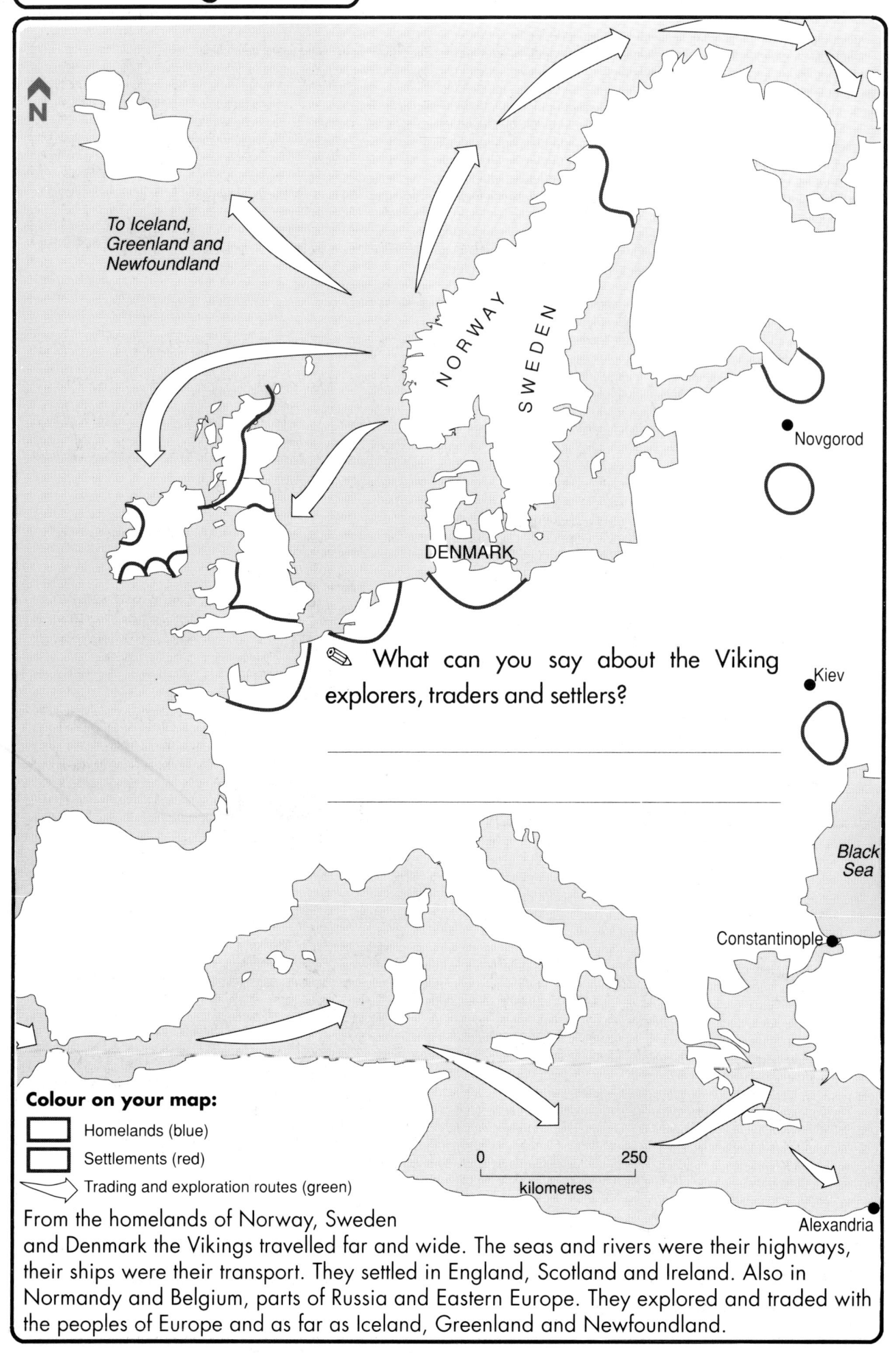

To Iceland, Greenland and Newfoundland

NORWAY
SWEDEN
DENMARK
Novgorod
Kiev
Black Sea
Constantinople
Alexandria

✎ What can you say about the Viking explorers, traders and settlers?

_____

_____

Colour on your map:
☐ Homelands (blue)
☐ Settlements (red)
➔ Trading and exploration routes (green)

0   250
kilometres

From the homelands of Norway, Sweden and Denmark the Vikings travelled far and wide. The seas and rivers were their highways, their ships were their transport. They settled in England, Scotland and Ireland. Also in Normandy and Belgium, parts of Russia and Eastern Europe. They explored and traded with the peoples of Europe and as far as Iceland, Greenland and Newfoundland.

Viking Dress

There are a number of **sources** we can turn to that show us what the Vikings looked like. Some of these are shown in the table below.

Viking sagas (stories written at the time which describe Viking costume)	1	2	3	4	5
Picture stones (Viking men and women carved in stone)	1	2	3	4	5
Fragments of tapestry and embroidery	1	2	3	4	5
Grave goods, particularly when a body was buried fully clothed	1	2	3	4	5

✎ Which do you think are the most **reliable**? Draw a ring around a number in each case

1 = least reliable
5 = most reliable

✎ These 2 figures are dressed in typical Viking costume. All the jewellery, ornaments and objects have been found by archaeologists. Draw arrows to identify the description with the object.

Hair was tied up in a scarf.

Bracelets were popular.

Long linen pleated garment with short sleeves. A draw string held it round the neck.

Woollen over tunic.

Between the brooches were strung beads (amber, gold, silver and glass).

Hanging from a chain from one brooch would be personal objects like a knife, comb, keys.

Men wore a cap.

A tunic was worn over a shirt reaching to mid-thigh and held with a belt.

From the belt hung objects such as a knife, comb or purse.

Trousers were worn held up by a draw string.

Cloaks were worn, fastened on the shoulder with a clasp or brooch.

A man's most important possessions would have been his weapons.

Shoes and boots were made of leather.

In Viking society we hear a lot about the men, but it was women who ran the household and held the keys to the house. However 50 per cent of women died by the age of 35 and 55 was a good age to reach!!

Your Move Snarri!

This is a Viking board game that was played on winter's evenings in smoky halls. It is a game of attack and defence called HNEFATFAL (you pronounce each letter). The attackers have 24 pieces, the defenders have 13 pieces including the king called the HNEFI. It is his aim to escape to the edge of the board. The attackers win if they can surround him on all four sides.

How to play ......

Play with two sets of coloured counters. You will need 24 of one colour and 13 of another. The King's counter starts in the centre of the board. Mark this counter with an H for HNEFI! The defenders go on the squares shown by the spears, and the attackers go on the squares shown by the swords.
Maybe your class could have a championship.

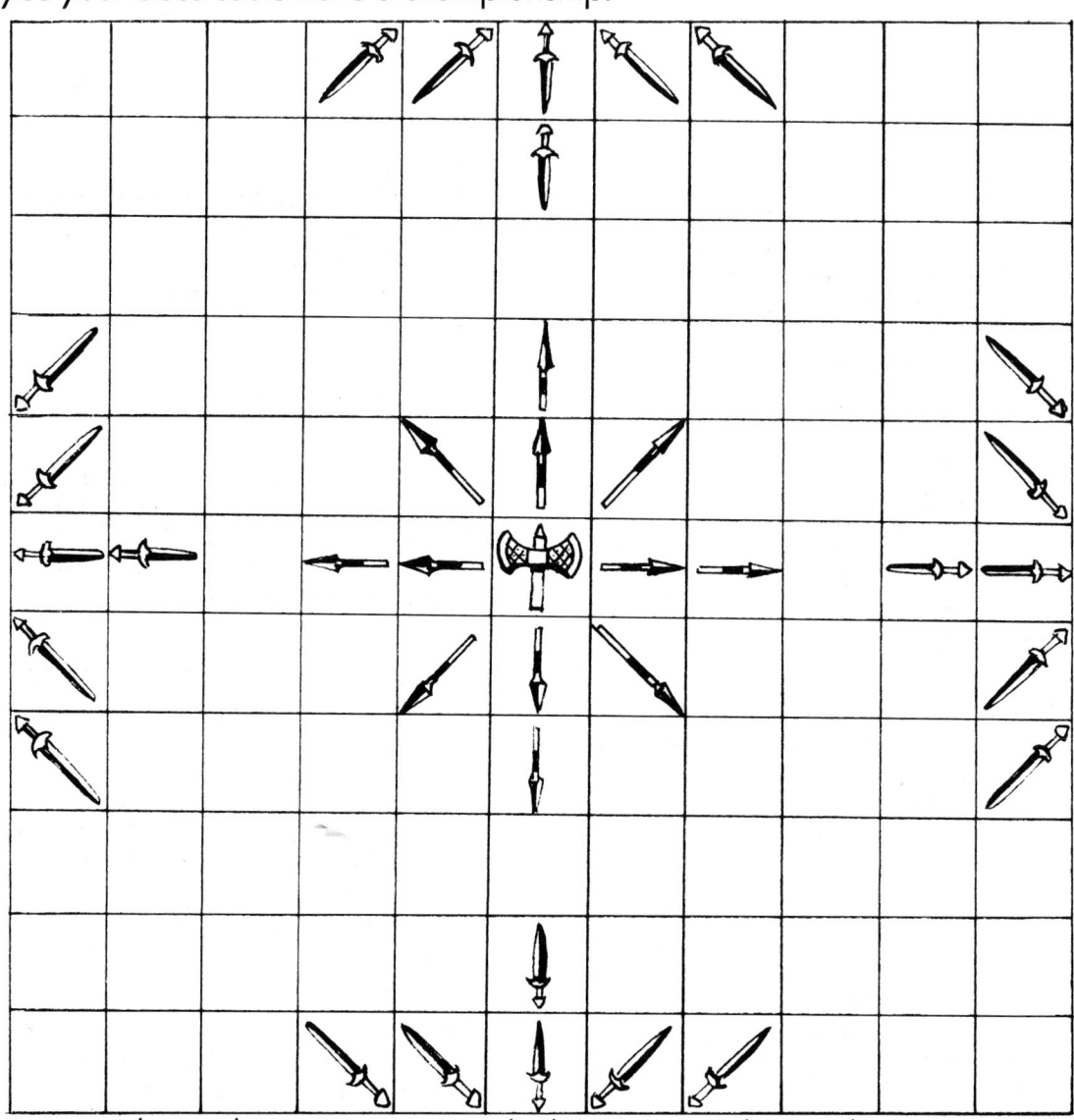

Players take it in turns to move and only one piece can be moved at a time.
The HNEFI's army moves first.
Pieces may move horizontally and vertically any number of places. No piece may move diagonally.
No two pieces may occupy the same square.
You may not jump over pieces.
To capture and remove your enemy from the board you must 'sandwich' his piece between 2 of your own.

© 1990 Folens Limited   This page may be photocopied for classroom use only

Ship Shapes

The most famous Viking ship discoveries were found in Roskilde Fiord. Archaeologists think that in the year 1 000 A.D. the channel of the fiord was blocked, probably deliberately, as a defence against enemies. Five ships were discovered. They had been stripped of their contents. Stakes had been driven into the boats to stop them drifting in the current and many had been filled with stones. The archaeologists discovered that each ship was different.

Wreck 1
A knorr. A heavy cargo ship. Decks **fore** and **aft** and an open **hold**. It would have had a single square sail. The bottom of the hull was smooth suggesting it stayed afloat rather than being pulled up on a beach.
16.5 metres long and 4.8 metres wide.

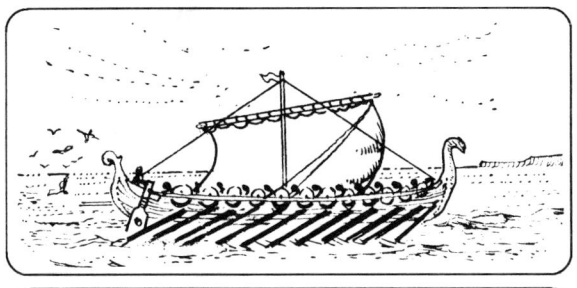

Wreck 2
A longship. A warship carrying 50 to 60 men. It was the longest Viking ship ever found. The ship was in a poor condition with many of its planks missing possibly to repair other ships.
28 metres long and 4.5 metres wide.

Wreck 3
A cargo vessel. Smaller than the knorr (Wreck 1). Oar holes showed it could be rowed to manoeuvre the vessel in narrow creeks. The hull was scraped showing it had been beached many times.
13.5 metres long and 3.2 metres wide.

Wreck 4
A small shallow vessel. It was probably a ferry or a fishing boat. It had a small sail and could have been rowed. Vikings would have learned to use boats like this from a very early age.
12 metres long and 2.5 metres wide.

Wreck 5
A warship. The ship had a complete deck and a rack for shields. There were 12 oar holes on either side and the hull had been patched many times.
18 metres long and 2.6 metres wide.

✂ Cut out these cards and try to match each description with the right picture.

Viking Homes

Anglo Saxon Chronicle 876 A.D.

"This year Healfdene shared out Northumbrian land, and they were ploughing and providing for themselves."

This entry in the chronicle suggests that the Vikings had come to stay.

What sort of houses did they live in?

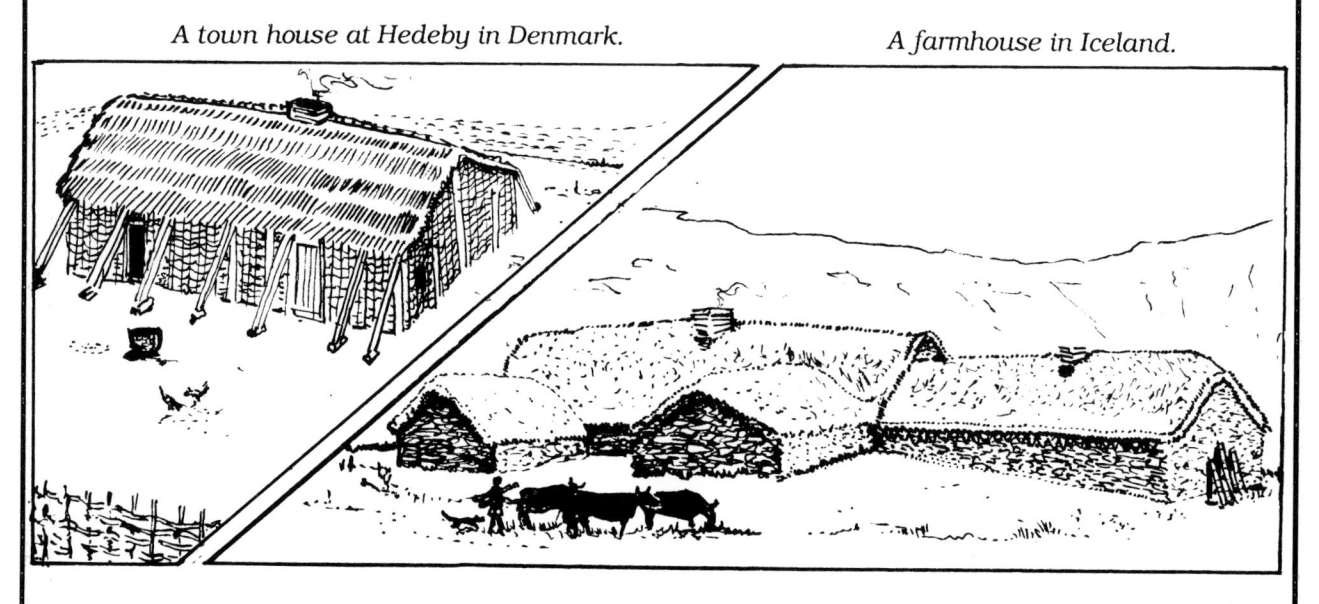

A town house at Hedeby in Denmark.

A farmhouse in Iceland.

Like all buildings, local materials were used - stone, timber, wattle and daub, thatch and turf for roofs.

✎ Draw a sketch of your home here:

✎ Make a list of 10 differences between your house and the Viking house.

A Viking Feast!

How do we know what sorts of things the Vikings liked to eat?

The excavations at Jorvic (Viking for York) have revealed many interesting remains which provide clues.

List of things found in excavation	What made up the Viking diet?
Cattle bones	
Pig bones	
Sheep bones	
Goat bones	
Chicken bones	
Geese bones	
Fish bones (freshwater and seawater)	
Cockle shells	
Oyster shells	
Vegetables - carrots, celery and beans	
Cereals - oats, barley, wheat and rye	
Fruits - apple pips, plum stones and blackberry pips	
Hazlenut shells	

✎ Use the evidence above to prepare a feast for a Viking chief!

Starter: _____

Main meal: _____

Sweet: _____

Drink: _____

© 1990 Folens Limited   This page may be photocopied for classroom use only

Viking Picture Stones

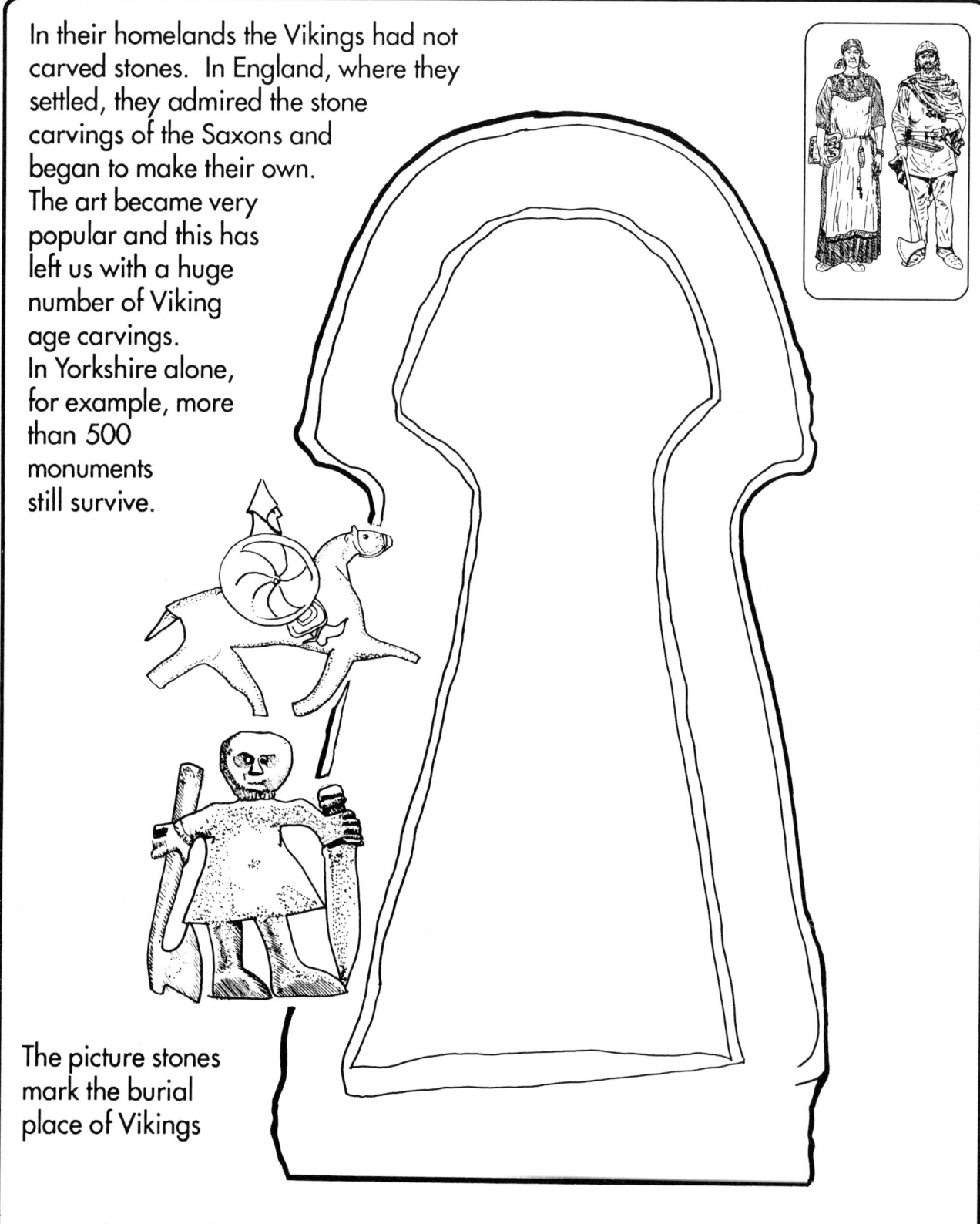

In their homelands the Vikings had not carved stones. In England, where they settled, they admired the stone carvings of the Saxons and began to make their own. The art became very popular and this has left us with a huge number of Viking age carvings. In Yorkshire alone, for example, more than 500 monuments still survive.

The picture stones mark the burial place of Vikings

✎ What sort of Viking do you think these stones mark?

✎ Design a stone for yourself. The picture should show what sort of person you are!
OR
Design a stone for a Viking - a seafarer?, a farmer?, a warrior?, a craftsman?

The stones often had decorated borders and were brightly coloured.

© 1990 Folens Limited   This page may be photocopied for classroom use only

Countdown to Invasion 1066 .....

Edward died on January 6th 1066. This immediately plunged England into turmoil. Who would be the new king?
There were 3 rivals who all believed they had the right to the crown. All three men were very powerful.

Harold - Earl of Wessex • Harald Hardrada - A Danish King • William - Duke of Normandy

■ Read these descriptions and try to decide who is who.

A. This man claimed he was King of Denmark and Norway. He felt that as the Danes had conquered England he should also be King of England.

B. This man claimed that Edward had promised him the throne. He also claimed that when Harold had been shipwrecked off Normandy he had sworn on holy relics that he would help him become King of England.

C. This man was English and the most powerful man in the land. England needed a strong ruler and he was an excellent soldier. The English Council, called the Witan, also wanted him.

✎ Who do you think had the best claim to the throne of England and why?

_____

_____

_____

"Earl Harold was crowned King and he had little peace during the time he ruled the Kingdom."

Anglo Saxon Chronicle

■ The Bayeux tapestry takes up the story. Look at this episode .....

■ Try to find:

▼ Harold sitting on his throne. What do you think he is being told?
▼ The Witan pointing to a comet. What do you think they are saying to each other?
▼ The ghostly ships in the border. What do you think they mean?

© 1990 Folens Limited   This page may be photocopied for classroom use only

Invasion 1066!

Of course William was furious when he heard that Harold had been crowned King of England. It had been promised to him.

✎ Plot the chain of events that led to the fatal invasion of England on your map. They are listed below in **chronological** order. Use pictures, symbols, arrows as you wish!

1. Harold, fed up with waiting for the invasion, disbands his fleet in August 1066.

2. September 1066. Harald Hardrada invades the North of England with 300 ships and reaches York.

3. King Harold marches North from London to meet the Vikings.

4. 25th September 1066. Two miles south of York at Stamford Bridge - King Harold destroys the Viking army.

5. Duke William of Normandy and the Norman Invasion army land at Pevensey near Hastings. 27-28th September 1066.

6. Harold receives news of the Invasion and, marches his tired army back to Hastings.

7. Hastings. October 14th 1066. Harold and William's armies face each other .....

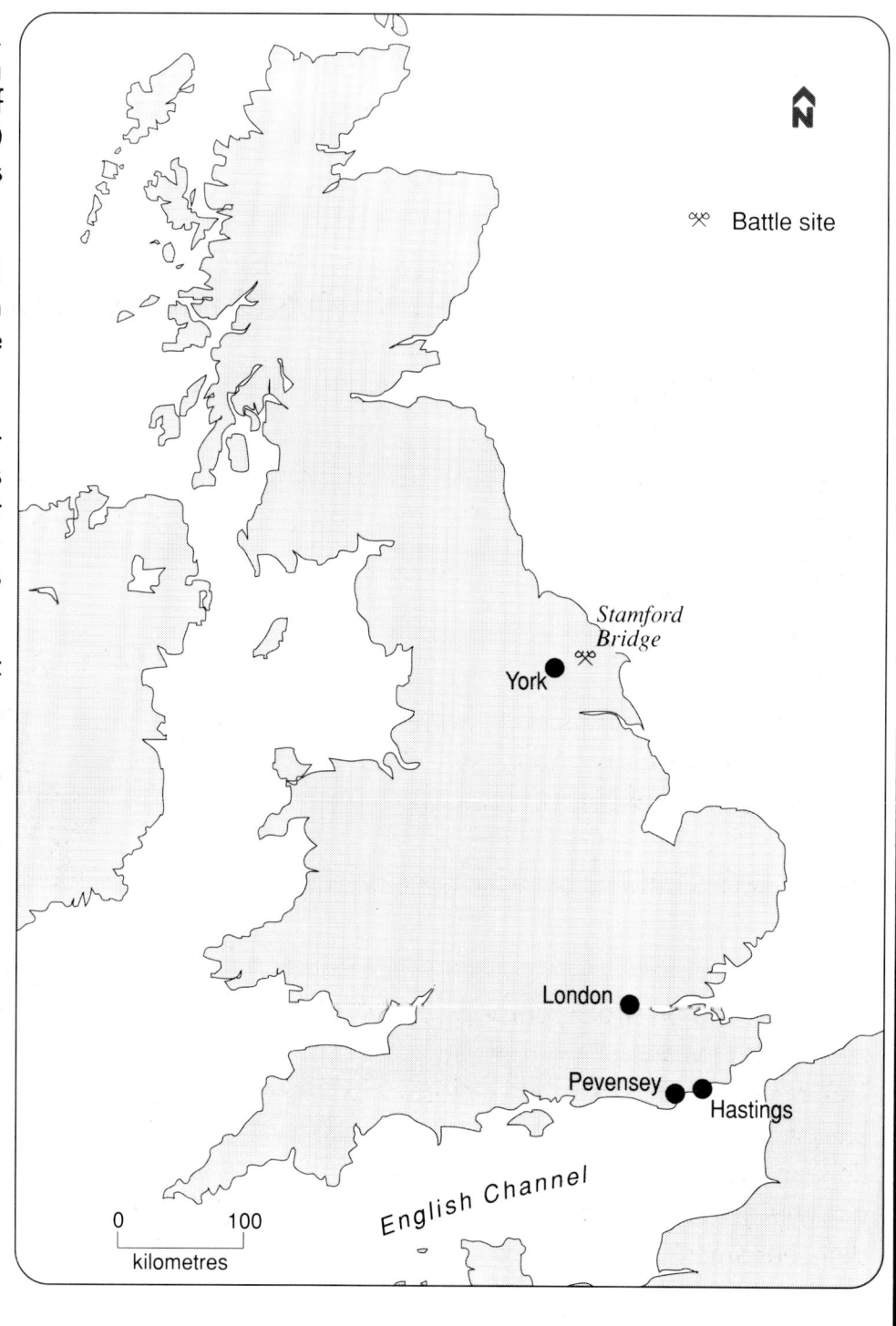

⚔ Battle site

© 1990 Folens Limited   This page may be photocopied for classroom use only

Saxon versus Norman: Hastings 1066

On October 14 1066 Harold and William's armies face each other at Hastings .....

The Saxon HOUSECARL was the best fighting man in Europe in 1066. The Bayeux embroidery shows us how they looked.

✎ Describe their weapons and clothes.

The Norman Knight made up the bulk of William's army.

✎ Describe a Knight - and how he is different from the Housecarl?

One of the final battle scenes from the Bayeux embroidery tells us what happened to Harold! The caption above the two Saxons says "HERE KING HAROLD IS KILLED" - but which one is Harold?

hAROLD:REX:INTERFEC
TVS:EST

One seems to be struck, perhaps in the eye, by an arrow.
The other is cut down by a Norman knight.
Perhaps both men are Harold - two pictures of the same man shown at two different times!

Research Try to find out for yourself what happened in the battle!

■ What do you think?

Putting it in the Right Order

This is a game to see if you can understand **who** and **what** came **where** and **when** in the historical period covered by the units in this book.

✂ Cut out all 10 pictures and mount them onto card.

1. Jumble the cards and put them face down in a pile. Take the top 2 cards. Which card comes first in the pair or could they be from the same time?
2. Now try it with 3 cards. Where does the third card go?
3. Play 'pick up pairs' with a partner. Lay all 10 cards before you face down and match pairs. When you have found a pair you may keep them until all the pairs are found.

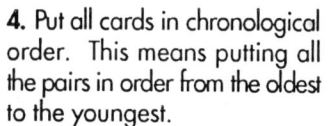

4. Put all cards in chronological order. This means putting all the pairs in order from the oldest to the youngest.
5. Make 4 more cards. On each card write one of the following:
2 500 years ago   900 years ago   1 500 years ago   2 000 years ago.
Which picture cards go with the new cards (the Saxons and Vikings lived at roughly the same time)?
6. Historians often talk of B.C. (Before Christ) or A.D. (Anno Domini - 'In the year of our Lord').
Which cards would you group with B.C. and which with A.D.? (Be careful with the Romans!)
7. Of all the invading and settling people of the British Isles which you have studied, which period would you have liked to live in and why?

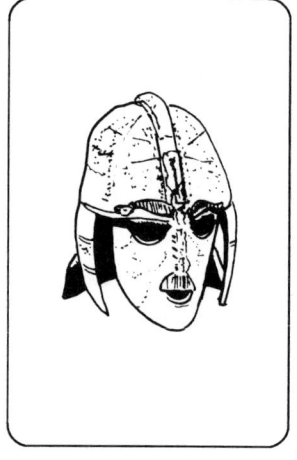

© 1990 Folens Limited   This page may be photocopied for classroom use only